Contents

Acknowledgements

I was fortunate in being able to persuade a number of people to talk about their experiences as interviewers. This allowed me to check what is currently being done in a variety of organizations both against 'good practice' as suggested by the Institute of Personnel Management and against my own experiences.

The people who gave their time and thoughts so willingly were: Susie Bray, Senior Personnel Officer, Heart of England Building Society; Paula Brown, Personnel Officer, Rackhams (House of Fraser); Tony Goldsby, Operations Director, Listgrove Limited, International & National Recruitment Consultants; Jean Holder, District Councillor and retired Head Teacher; Penny Holdsworth, Managing Director, Holdsworth Recruitment Agency; Oona Hudson, Assistant Personnel Officer, Civilian Staff Recruitment, Warwickshire County Constabulary; Pat Jones, Head of Human Resources, Heart of England Building Society; Sangita Kakad, Lecturer in Sociology and Equal Opportunities Coordinator, Mid-Warwickshire College of Further Education; Angela Pocock, Personnel Officer, Warwickshire County Council; Sylvia Shimmin, Visiting Professor, University of Leeds; Alex Sproat, Assistant Registrar, Personnel, University of Warwick; Keith Talbot, Police Recruitment Officer, Warwickshire County Constabulary; David Thompson, Manager, Assessment Services, The Post Office; Lois I. Whittaker, Personnel and Training Manager, Institute of Personnel Management. I am also grateful for the contacts made for me by Roger Farrance, President of the Institute of Personnel Management.

I also waylaid numerous people – friends, associates and passing acquaintances – and asked them about their experiences of being interviewed.

I must, however, stress that the views expressed in this book are my own. If I have used anything provided by any of the people I have spoken to, this has been acknowledged in the text and I trust I have not distorted their ideas too badly.

I could not end the acknowledgements without mentioning the financial and psychological support given by my wife whilst I was writing the book. Praise be for working wives who are good at being interviewed!

SUCCEED AT YOUR JOB INTERVIEW

George Heaviside

BBC BOOKS

Published by BBC Books,
a division of BBC Enterprises Limited,
Woodlands, 80 Wood Lane, London W12 0TT

First published 1993

ISBN 0 563 36742 3

Typeset in Monotype Times by
Ace Filmsetting Ltd, Frome, Somerset

Printed and bound in Great Britain by
Redwood Press Limited, Melksham, Wiltshire

Cover printed by Clays Ltd, St Ives Plc

Quick reference information finder

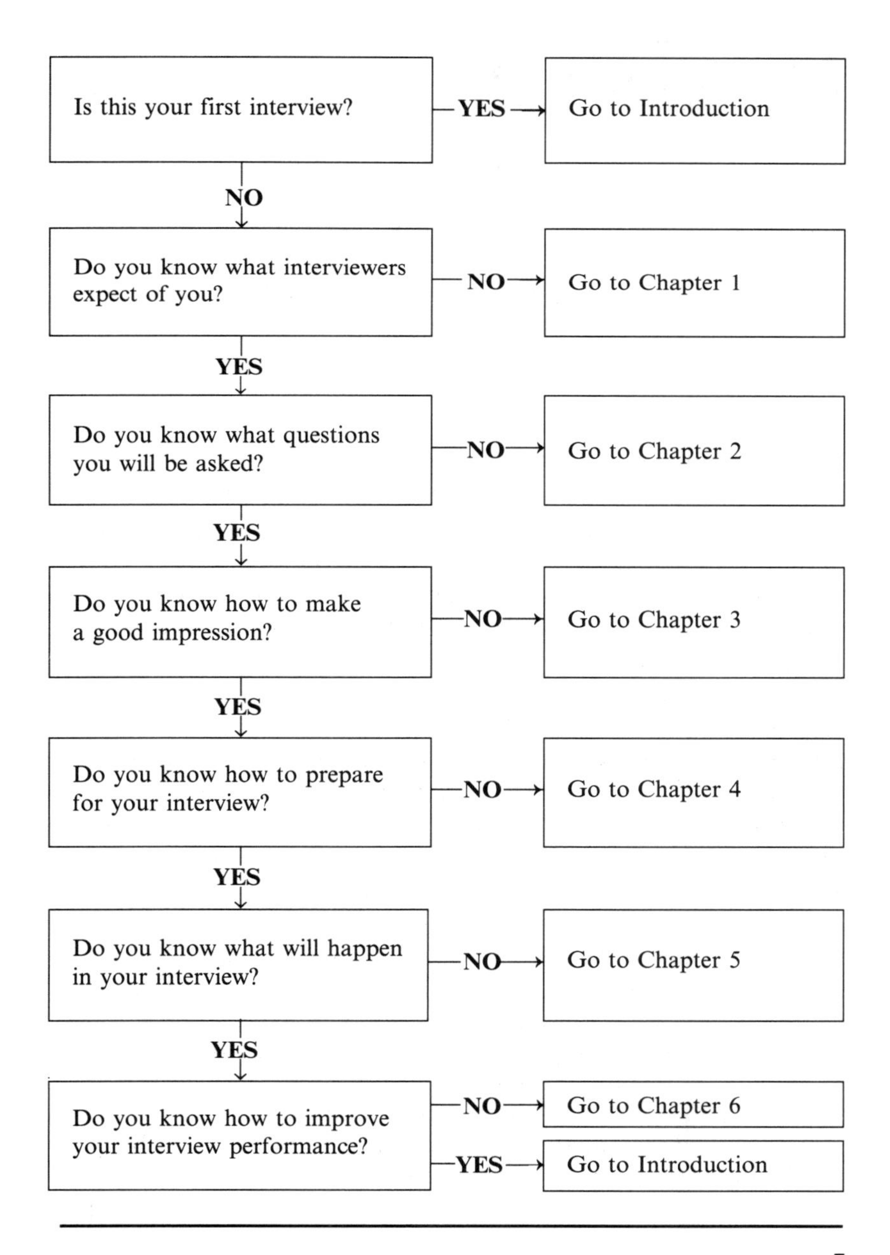

Introduction

'All the world's a stage,
And all the men and women merely players . . .
And one man in his time plays many parts.'

As You Like It, Act II, Scene VII
William Shakespeare

What is it in modern society which is the largest cause of stress when we have it and the largest cause of stress when we don't?

That's right – it's work! That's what surveys reported in the press from time to time tell us. It must also be a great source of satisfaction - why else would we stick at it for about forty per cent of our lives? We need it as much as organizations need us to do it.

In the 1950s if someone was breathing, walking and had their P45 they could get a job. With only half a million people 'unemployed', even the 'unemployable' got jobs. In the 1980s we were told that demographic changes would reduce the number of people available for work. This was forecast as a shortage of young people which would be at its worst by the mid 1990s. But look about you – forecasters are not always right. There is no prediction without error.

The reality in our society at the start of the 1990s is different. How often have you been one of the 100 people who apply for a job, fortunate enough to be one of the ten who are interviewed and one of the unlucky nine who get the 'Dear . . .' letter? If this is the pattern of your job applications, then you will benefit from reading this book. If, like the majority of us, your track record of success at getting jobs is somewhat patchy, then read on. Whether you are about to embark on your first serious job interview or have few problems in getting interviews but just seem to fall at the last hurdle, there are plenty of ideas inside for you.

This book has been written on the assumptions that:

- Your life and career depend upon getting and keeping jobs in which you can express your abilities and obtain personal, material and psychological satisfaction.
- Less satisfying work causes stress which can spin off into your non-work activities and may depress you.
- Satisfying work can elevate your life totally at work and outside of it because work is strongly related to your status in society and your feelings of personal worth and self esteem.
- You may not naturally be good at presenting yourself in the best possible light in the typically short space of time devoted to interviews by many organizations.
- A small investment in improving your self-presentation skills can produce a disproportionately large increase in the end result: with a little advice and practice you can achieve greater control, more self-confidence and project a more accurate picture of yourself as an individual and a prospective employee.
- You should try to take as much control of your life as possible if you want to be a 'winner'.
- Getting suitable work is a competitive activity which entails three things:
  - knowing a great deal about yourself as a commodity which has a value in the world of work,
  - understanding 'buyers' - the organizations which cannot fulfil their purpose without people,
  - being good at self-presentation - the ways in which you can persuade organizations to use your skills.

My aim is to help you to review and build upon your ways of preparing for and succeeding in the face-to-face job interview. It is the most popular method of selecting people for work - and thus one at which we all need to be able to give our 'best shot'.

I am assuming you have decided upon the direction(s) in life you wish to pursue. If so, we can focus our efforts on your desire to exert a greater influence over the decisions which are being made during your interview. These may be interviews which you have gained after replying to advertised vacancies, those where you have persuaded organizations to ask you along to discuss the possibility of working for them as well as those concerned with promotion or career development.

This practical 'self-marketing' approach is based on many years of work with employed and unemployed people from late teens to late fifties, from various backgrounds, organizations and occupational levels, male and female, executive, managerial, supervisory, skilled and manual, first-time job seekers and 'old hands'. They were all seeking to develop their careers and improve their interview skills. For most it helped boost their self-confidence. For some it confirmed that their common-sense approach to self-presentation was good practice and would work if they persevered conscientiously and 'polished up' their technique. Everyone increased their knowledge about and range of practical interviewee skills.

I have chosen to personalise this approach by writing it in the third person - as if I was talking directly to you. I have tried to avoid jargon but have scattered colloquialisms and anecdotes liberally amongst the text.

The chapter titles are rhetorical: they pose and answer fundamental questions. The first is concerned with what the 'buyers' - organizations and interviewers - are seeking. We then move on to the type of questions you will be asked and the ways in which they might be posed and could be answered. In Chapter 3 we review how you can start to overcome the 'customer objections' outlined in Chapter 1 and show how to make a good first impression. Chapter 4 looks at ways of preparing and rehearsing for your interview. Several different approaches to interviews and how they are conducted are covered in Chapter 5, which also looks at strategies which many larger organizations are now using to supplement the more traditional interview. Finally, in Chapter 6, we look at ways of coping with interviews where you felt you didn't do so well and how you can improve your performance.

Self-assessment questionnaires, exercises and checklists are included to help you understand yourself, develop and polish your interview techniques and act as 'refreshers' when doing your preparation.

However great or small the improvement you need to 'Succeed At Your Job Interview', I am sure you'll find some useful ideas in here. Good luck.

1 What are interviewers looking for?

'My train are men of choice that all particulars of duty know.'

King Lear Act I, Scene IV
William Shakespeare

Organizations spend a great deal of time and money preparing for your interview. They analyse work to develop a job description and derive a personnel specification, seek suitable internal applicants, advertise and/or use external sources, scan hundreds of pieces of paper, shortlist and undertake many other administrative activities. By the time of the interview they will not only have a profile of their 'ideal' candidate, whom they believe will be able to succeed at the job in question, but also an impression of you. What sort of person walks through the door of the interview room?

This chapter considers some of the expectations interviewers have of you and their criticisms of what you actually do during an interview. These will be reviewed in some depth, alternative ways of dealing with them suggested and a number of action points developed for you to use in your preparation.

What expectations do interviewers have?

The Polytechnic of Wales surveyed all the companies in their area employing over 200 people. They provided each organization with a list of 20 personal and educational factors and asked them to rate them in order of importance when selecting school leavers.

The following table shows each factor in terms of the percentages thought to be (1) Very or Quite Important and (2) Important. The balancing percentage of responses all come under the Not Very Important Category, which has not been shown.

	Percentages	
Factor	*Very or Quite Important*	*Important*
Reliability and trustworthiness	91	7
Punctuality	91	9
Willingness to learn	88	9
Ability to work as team member	85	14
Enthusiasm	82	17
Clean and tidy appearance	78	20
Ability to work with minimal supervision	61	33
Initiative	59	34
Ability to work with figures	56	30
Ability to write clearly and concisely	52	38
Well organized	52	42
Ability to speak fluently/confidently	51	40
Friendliness	44	44
Some qualifications related to job	35	22
Good O levels/GCSEs in academic subjects	30	31
Qualifications in vocational subjects	23	36
Good dress sense	23	38
Some general work experience	23	22
Creativity	22	46
Work experience related to job	21	16

An analysis of numerous attributes sought by people who recruit graduates for academic positions resulted in the following four areas:

Achievement motivation
Being well informed about the organization
Quality of references
Academic performance

Company interviewers rated the last two attributes much lower than do academics.

If you are neither a school leaver nor an undergraduate you will be more interested in other sources of information. The content of selection interview training programmes, analyses of interviews and discussions with professional and occasional interviewers suggest that the following factors are assessed most frequently during interviews.

Assertiveness
Emotional stability
Enthusiasm
Good personal appearance
Good educational record
Honesty and moral standards
Humility
Interest in people
Leadership potential
Long-range plans and objectives formulated
Motivation
Oral communication skills
Participation in outside activities
Pleasant first impression
Poise during interview
Prepared for the interview - knows the company
Realistic salary expectations
Relevant work experience
Self-confidence
Use of initiative
Willingness to travel
Written skills

These are in not in order of importance as this ultimately depends upon the job description and the person profile.

Whether you are a school leaver, a college graduate or an older person, there are factors common to these lists of interest to everyone. To what extent do you feel able to live up to these?

What are interviewers' criticisms?

They say you:

- Don't prepare.
- Make negative statements about yourself and your experiences.
- Make derogatory remarks about the organization, the interviewers or the procedures and show bitterness towards others.

- Are poorly motivated.
- Have poor face-to-face communication skills.

What they mean is:

■ ***You are insufficiently prepared***

You will not have thought about the job, the person who could succeed at it and about yourself in relation to these. You will have given little or no thought to the organization, nor will there be any indication that you have thought about how you see your career developing or the sort of questions you would like to put to the interviewers. Furthermore, the way in which you answer questions adds to the overall picture of someone who appears to have done nothing beforehand other than simply read the invitation and arrive. All of this lack of preparation and interest becomes obvious to the interviewers and makes it increasingly unlikely that you will succeed.

Here are four specific examples of ways in which you respond and some thoughts and advice on how you might deal with similar questions in the future:

1 'I can't really remember . . .'
Perhaps you need time to think, so what do you do? Repeat or re-phrase the question by saying something like: 'Are you saying . . . ?' Or perhaps you stall for a little time by looking pensively downwards, wrinkling your brow, averting your eyes from the questioner and then look up at them and say 'Can I just have a couple of seconds to think about that one?', by which time you should have something pertinent and positive to contribute. Even if you can't remember, don't say it.

2 'That's a bit tricky for me to say . . .'
Of course some of their questions are going to be tricky. Interviews are tests and not every question is going to be answered by you giving a recital of factual information. Perhaps something like: 'I've never come across that before . . . but what I might/would think/feel/do is . . .'.

3 'I have 22 people working for me, or is it 26 . . . ?'
They won't know exactly how many people work for you so state a figure confidently and leave it at that. Try to be consistent and

use the same figure again. Alternatively, give two figures – '. . . between 22 and 26 people. It varies according to the work and how many contract staff I have.' Think of a plausible reason, say it confidently and the interviewers will not usually challenge you if it is a minor point.

4 'I can't answer that. I've never really thought about it . . .'
NO! Never refuse to answer is such a bald way. They want you to think about it – NOW. That's why they're asking - to see if you can think on your feet – or rather your seat. So what do you say? Forget the '. . . can't answer . . .' bit and try: 'I've never come across that situation but what I think I might do/feel/say is . . .'. You might even turn it around quickly and try the reflecting-back approach: 'Do you mean/are you talking about . . . ?' and re-phrase or just ask them outright for some more information.

■ ***You make negative value judgements about yourself and your experiences***

This means you put yourself down. Please don't do it. This criticism may well arise because you really do have this negative attitude towards yourself. However, it is more likely the result of not having thought through some of the more predictable questions which you may be asked and ways in which you could respond to them. You are caught 'off balance' too often by the unexpected and respond in a defensive or negative way. Some interviewers are just looking for the slightest opportunity to mark you down and make any initial poor impression (or prejudice) come true. Don't make negative value judgements about yourself or your experiences. State the facts and let them evaluate what you supply. By introducing negative judgement you put them into an unfavourable frame of mind: you predispose them to think badly of you and your track record. How do you know that what you have done is less than they are looking for? It could be too much or just right. Don't go along with their negative judgements about you or your track record. Here are six examples to think about:

1 'I find getting on with people a little difficult.'
Who doesn't at some time or another? Do you mean all people or just some? Don't you find some people impossible to relate to? There's nothing wrong with that. But don't make sweeping generalisations. Perhaps you need to think about a specific, more

acceptable response such as: 'I must say that I find it a bit difficult when someone promises me something and then lets me down by not keeping their promise on time.' You must be able to justify your statement. Think through some things that you dislike in relationships which are generally understood and acceptable.

2 'I had a personality clash with . . .'
This may well be a 'top of the head' reply to questions such as: 'How do you get along with people?', 'What sort of people do you find it difficult to relate to?', 'When was the last time you had a good argument with someone?'. These are predictable questions probing your interpersonal relationships and tolerance threshold which may be very important in some jobs. Find a socially acceptable response. What does annoy you which you can put across in a fairly adult and rational way – and which probably annoys interviewers as well? Perhaps 'There was a member of the team who always seemed to find fault with/resist new ideas/rarely seemed to see any good in other people's ideas . . .' You must be prepared to elaborate on whatever response you have chosen.

3 'Someone better than me was appointed over my head.'
Never say this! It probably happens to thousands of people so don't use that as a reply to a question such as 'Why were you not appointed?' So what else can you try? Well, you can be open and say something like: 'I had a go but obviously the panel thought I needed some further experience compared with some of the other candidates and now I am trying to get that . . .' or whatever you feel is more acceptable. (If it really has happened to you, then you need to seek some feedback from others about positive things you could do to put yourself in a better position for promotion in the future. Perhaps you do have some areas which need developing. No one is perfect. Treat such situations as opportunities to learn about yourself, do something and grow.)

Undervaluing your experiences is another aspect of this syndrome of self-denigration. The sort of thing you might say is:

4 'I'm only a . . . (job title/status/whatever).'
No human being is 'only'. You are what you are so never devalue yourself. Remove this dreadful word from your vocabulary – certainly for the duration of any interview. State what you are and

don't be negative about it. If you don't feel good about something in your life, then what are you doing about it?

5 'My industrial relations experiences are limited to . . .'
You're at it again. Tell them what you have done, not what you have not done, and don't make negative comments about it. Say: 'Well as far as IR goes, I have . . . and . . . as well as . . .' Let them dig deeper if they want to, and be prepared for it.

6 'My project was fairly simple.'
As above. Give them the facts. Let them probe. Your project management experience may have been limited but could be a sound basis for taking on bigger and better things with them.

Some interviewers are very adept at putting you down. Research evidence suggests that they often look for reasons to support their initial negative pre-judgements rather than seeking a balanced view of you. You must not deliberately load their guns for them. Do not devalue or undervalue yourself or your experience.

Winners don't whinge.

- ***'You make derogatory remarks about the organization, the interviewers or the procedures and show bitterness towards others'***

This is another example of lack of preparation, inability to deal with the unexpected and a possible underlying frustration – all of which can be overcome. You have to be careful of falling into the trap of rejecting all or part of the recruitment, selection or interviewing procedure. The organization has designed it – however 'patchy' you might think it is – to serve their purposes. Think about the following four examples – and avoid making this type of mistake:

1 'In my opinion psychological tests are unimportant.'
Well, 'Thank you and goodbye' might be the unspoken reaction of some interviewers. The better ones will come back immediately with something like: 'That's an interesting point of view, tell us about it.' If you are going to criticise something, then you've got to have your rational arguments at the ready. You could well turn a dangerous loser situation into something more positive. There are pros and cons in most things and you should be able to see both sides of the argument.

2 'I would have thought my CV says it all . . .'
Can't you just hear an arrogant candidate saying this? You've put down the whole of their procedure and them as well. They've invested hours of their precious time and thousands of pounds to get you to where you are – and you criticise their 'baby'. You are leaving yourself wide open for a full frontal attack – in as nice a way as possible of course: 'What exactly is it, you feel, that your CV is telling us?' And now you're really on the spot. If you can't make this into an opportunity to sell yourself, there is a hard uphill struggle ahead for you when it ought not to have happened.

3 'I was hoping to see someone more senior.'
Do you wonder why you never get to a final interview? Whatever your feelings are about the way in which you are treated, you should avoid attacking the organization, the interviewers or the procedure you are going through. If necessary, take an assertive approach and let them understand your point of view without becoming aggressive. You may wish to take up your points of disagreement afterwards, in writing at a higher level. Showing bitterness towards others could be part of a 'biting the hand that fed/feeds you' syndrome. Don't do it. If there are things still gnawing away at you years after they happened, then find some way of talking them out of your system – it's unhealthy to have a chip on your shoulder for too long.

4 'It was the MD's fault, he . . .'
Organizations want problem solvers and not problem bringers. If you are going to say that to strangers about your present/last boss, then what's to stop you saying it about them? If you are always seeing other people as the cause of your ill-fortune, then you should take a long hard look at yourself in the mirror – especially before any interviews. If you aren't part of the solution you must be part of the problem. Try to come up smelling of roses: 'Perhaps some of the decisions taken at the top, on reflection, were not the best. But I can understand perhaps why they were taken. I feel everyone has learned from that mistake.' Or are you perfect compared with everyone else?

■ ***'You lack motivation'***

This is often the overall impression you create and which the interviewers have inferred from behaviour such as your apathy, desultory replies to questions and your disinterest in developing them. You may give monosyllabic replies and miss or fail to make opportunities to 'promote' or 'sell' yourself. The impression is that you do not know what you want out of life, where your career lies and how this job fits into your aspirations. There may also be a tendency for you to 'go along' with whatever the interviewers suggest or not to be able to put forward a reasoned case in the face of opposition from them.

In general, your total lack of enthusiasm comes through clearly. Why did you bother to apply? Why did you accept the invitation? Why is your heart not really in the procedure? Does failing not really matter to you? Why are you wasting your time and that of the organization and interviewers? If it's important, it's worth doing well. It takes very little to move you from being a disinterested tail-ender to a strong contender. Examine your motives when you apply for the job and accept their invitation. If you have any hesitation you will project it by your body language and your general demeanour.

If you are a candidate for an internal promotion, you must be wary of assuming that you will automatically get the job, that the interview is some form of 'lip service' to show that 'justice is being done' and favouritism is not influencing the organization's choice. It is true that often their preference is for 'the devil they know', but you shouldn't make the mistake of being complacent and not preparing yourself. Your desire to achieve even greater things cannot be realised if you don't get this job.

■ ***'You have poor communication skills'***

It could be, of course, that the impression you give of not having prepared or being poorly motivated is due to or magnified by your poor communication skills. This could mean that you talk too much or talk too little – or even not at all on occasions. Perhaps you don't get to the point and ramble on, or are poorly organized, evasive and give incomplete and inaccurate answers? You may even start to commandeer the conversation or go off on some pet 'hobby horse' of little interest to the interviewers. Do you allow your nerves to take over, forget the point you were making or use too much of your own 'jargon'?

From the above you will see that you may well be letting yourself down on several fronts - none of which represents an insuperable problem, provided you are prepared to work at them. Perhaps you are nervous and this interferes with your self-presentation skills? Preparation is the most practical way of reducing you nerves, enhancing your skills and improving your interview performance. Some of these criticisms could be interpreted as signs of immaturity, of unrealistic expectations, of an over-concern with 'What's in it for me?'. Your concern should firstly be for the 'buyer' – the organization in the form of the interviewer – and *then* for yourself.

The basic message is to make the interviewers' job easy and you make things easier for yourself. Interviewers are simply dying to select the 'right person' to work for them – and usually by yesterday. Therefore, your preparation rests upon overcoming their objections, meeting their expectations and trying to demonstrate you have the attributes and characteristics they seek – without trying to be all things to all men.

In summary, it appears that organizations are looking for well-prepared, thoughtful, positively motivated, energetic, enthusiastic and skilled communicators who are problem-solvers and not problem-bringers. Bear this in mind when doing your preparation before and presenting yourself at an interview.

2 What will they ask me?

'We have learned the answers, all the answers. It is the question that we do not know.'

The Hamlet of Archibald Macleish

The interviewers' major complaint is that you haven't prepared. This means you haven't thought about yourself, the job, the organization and type of questions you are likely to be asked. If your preparation concentrates on these you will increase your confidence, enhance your self-presentation and improve your chances of success. The focus in this chapter is on three aspects: what **areas** they will cover, what **questions** you are likely to be asked and which **questioning techniques** they will use.

The questioning areas

What interviewers know about you beforehand represents your 'skeleton'. What they are trying to do is to 'flesh out' these bare bones by discovering what makes you tick. What they do not have is an explanation of why you did what you did (i.e. your motivation) and how you felt about your experiences. They attempt to find out these aspects of your character by the type of questions they ask. You should try to tailor your responses to help them as much as you can.

If you want to know what questions you are likely to be asked, you need to think like an interviewer. This is not too difficult if they have been trained. If they have not, your task becomes a little more difficult, but don't despair. I said difficult – not impossible. However much training they have had, they need to explore two broad areas – your work experience and you as an individual. Analysing whatever information they have on you will help them to identify specific questioning areas they wish to pursue. They should prepare by reviewing the job description and personnel specification and any correspondence from you together with your application form(s), psychological test results and references where applicable. Thus it is possible to predict the broad areas of the questions you will be asked and, in some instances, the specific words they will use.

In general you will be asked biographical questions about your early life, education and qualifications, occupational training and work experiences, interests outside of school and work and your present circumstances. Interviewers will also wish to talk about the content of the job – how you match up to their specifications and what your views are on the job – and the context of the work itself – the working conditions and environment and how you feel about them.

Any perceived discrepancies between you and the job description and personnel specification will be broached. They will wish to explore the extent to which you have the experience, personal qualities, qualifications or training they require. If you do not match these closely, they will wish to see how any gaps might affect your suitability and will seek reassurance from you about how these can be resolved, without having an adverse impact on your job performance.

They may also probe any aspects of you, your life and career which they consider to be novel, unclear, strange or unattractive. They will wish to see whether or not you can satisfactorily explain them away, e.g. having had too many or too few jobs, several short stays with employers or missing periods in your CV, etc.

Less experienced interviewers may write down the actual questions they wish to ask. More skilled interviewers will realise that this is neither possible nor necessary and will not usually go to this detail. However, exceptions to this will be covered in Chapter 5. They are more likely to have noted or highlighted some areas they would like to discuss i.e. your track record and you as a person. As a minimum they may have developed a 'starter' question for each area. This will often be an open request such as 'What were the biggest influences on your early life?'

This is aimed at getting you talking about your background. You should treat it as an opportunity to produce a succinct and interesting response. They realise that once you are talking, many of their subsequent questions will arise from the dynamics of the conversation.

Most interviewers also seem to have their own little stock of favourite, idiosyncratic or 'catch' questions which may have no apparent bearing on anything at all connected with the job. Some of these they will have 'stolen' from other people with whom they have interviewed. Others will be questions asked of them and which they feel are worth repeating. These are often 'killers', which may be used to help the interviewers to put you down, maintain their shaky status and self-image and prove that you are unworthy of working for them or their organization. They may also believe that they are testing your ability to withstand stress and to think on your feet. There's not much you can do to predict these. You may acquire some examples of these during your career – and even stoop to using them yourself.

Fred was a Senior Engineer and Drawing Office Manager. He had two favourite questions which he invariably asked everyone he interviewed for drafting, design and engineering appointments, both internal or external candidates:

'You are driving along a country road on your way to an important meeting. Your boss is with you and you have less than half an hour to get to your destination. Suddenly one of your wheels falls off. The four retaining nuts must have come loose. You still have the wheel but you have lost all of the nuts and have no spares in your toolkit. What are you going to do to continue your journey and get yourself and your boss there on time?'

'Recent work on the pyramids using the most up-to-date measuring instruments revealed that their bases were perfectly flat. How could the Egyptian architects and builders have managed this without the sophisticated equipment only developed in later centuries?'

No doubt you will wish to work them out for yourself. But what might their answers tell an interviewer about an interviewee? Eventually everyone got to know the answers through the office grapevine. The frightening thing is that Fred supposedly made some rational judgements about the candidates based on whether or not they were able to answer these questions. I believe that some interviewers probably do have what one might call 'trick' questions. However strange or irrelevant you might think their questions are, try to imagine that they have a good reason for asking them, take them all seriously and do your best to answer them properly.

Rebecca was being interviewed for appointment as a PA to a Managing Director. The interview seemed to have been going quite well when he asked her:

'If I suddenly called you into my office and asked you to get me an elephant by tomorrow, what would you do?'

Well, how would you answer that one? What do you think the MD was getting at? Is it a fair question and how should you treat it? Presumably it is a test question to see how you would think on your feet. It's a fairly common sort of tactic. Interviewers also have 'tricky' or 'sticky' ones. Some are more predictable than others and we shall review some of them below.

Whilst some interviewers will prepare by using a biographical approach, others will use your application form as their 'prompt', after having noted or highlighted things they wish to pursue in depth. You could do worse than to use this is in your own preparation – if only to refresh your memory on what you included or excluded on each application form.

The questions

We shall now look at the biographical areas and reasons why an interviewer would want to ask questions about them. Under each area I have included some predictable questions with comments. Finally, more examples of the types of question often found under each heading are listed. There are hundreds of these, many of which are merely variations on themes and I shall only be scratching the surface. I'm sure that you will be able to add some more from your own experiences.

- ***Your early background***

This is where you started in life. It provides a datum point for measuring your progress. Your early days will have had a great impact on you – for better or for worse. You may feel that you have risen above any early disadvantages. Perhaps, on reflection, you realize you may not have capitalized on the gifts or 'silver spoon' with which you were born. Whatever you have done, it says something about you. Winners overcome early disadvantages.

You need to brush up on your facts and feelings about when and where you were born, the area you lived in, what your parent(s) did, size of family, birth order, family occupations, parental influences, family mobility, extended family, pre-school days, childhood illnesses and outstanding memories. A typical starter is:

'Tell me about your family/early days.'
This is an opportunity to talk about something you ought to know about! You should have a clear idea what you are going to say. They may pick you up on something and ask for clarification or for you to build upon what you have said. If you have an unusual family name, it might be used as an ice-breaker. Be prepared to say something positive and interesting about it. Perhaps they will move on to:

'How did you feel about these early days?'
And so you make some comments. For many people life is full of ups and downs. Why not mention both – particularly if you can show how you have learned from the downs and managed to pull yourself up by your bootstraps. Other questions under this heading could include:

How did you get on with your family?
How would you describe your father/mother?
What did your father/mother do for a living?
Overall, how would you describe your family/family circumstances?
Did you have any special responsibilities in the family?
Looking back, what things did you value most about your family?

In questioning these aspects, interviewers will make inferences about your personal values, motivation, ability, development of personality traits, relationships with others, early indications of interests, direction in life and career ambitions.

■ ***Education and qualifications***

This was your first opportunity to relate to a wider circle of people – older and younger children, peers, those in charge, etc. It indicates what educational opportunities you may have had and what you made of them. It was probably your first systematic experience of developing your innate abilities. You will have had to conform to and be compared against new standards of behaviour and achievement. Some indication of the extent to which you responded to competition with your peers can be assessed.

You will need to brush up your facts and feelings about schools attended, type, location, size, how chosen, what alternatives there were, method of entrance, years spent in each, stages and classes reached, subjects studied and why, with what success, strongest/weakest subjects and why, most/least preferred subjects and why, positions of responsibility held and how appointed, participation in your school's academic and sporting or social activities, participation in non-academic activities, positions held and how appointed, any special activities, languages acquired and fluency (written and spoken), relations with teaching staff, leadership responsibilities if any, examinations taken with what success, opportunities for self-development, e.g. coaching in sports, cadet forces, career guidance, reasons for changing direction/leaving, any special honours/privileges bestowed, what and why, most memorable things about schooldays.

If you are older, then the emphasis on this part of your life will be much less – but you still need to be on your toes for certain types of job interviews, e.g. work in the educational sector.

A typical starting statement is:

'Talk me though your education and qualifications.'
This is a standard approach – especially if you are a younger person, a graduate or someone with an unusual educational record. Then there is the adversarial approach:

'You don't seem to have done so well at school.'
This may be true and you may have a genuine reason for it – health, family circumstances – which you may or may not wish to talk about. Show how you have risen above this and it is no longer influential in your life. Play down any negative aspects. Try to select things which went well and try not to mention things which

did not. Jump to subsequent achievements. Other typical questions might include:

Which schools did you attend?
Why did you go to those particular schools?
At which subjects did you do best?
Did you achieve any special distinctions?
What were your favourite subjects at school?
What sort of responsibilities did you have in school?
How satisfying were your schooldays now you look back?
What sort of results did you get during termtime and in exams?
Which subject did you not like so much or not do so well in?
What sports or non-academic activities did you participate in?
What would you do differently if you were going to start again?
Who was the most influential teacher you met at school and why?
How useful would you say your schooldays have been in your life generally?
What would you say was the most outstanding recollection from your school days?

Questioning you about this area provides indications of how you developed your intellectual ability, the further development of your personality, broadening of interests, desire to seek wider opportunities, ability to relate to an increasing range of strangers, embryonic leadership opportunities, ability to deal with pressure, the self-discipline needed to progress studies (often unaided), etc. Where results of psychometric tests (paper and pencil tests which determine your aptitudes, attainments and personality) are available, comparisons will be made between what (partially) inherited abilities you have against the ways in which you applied them. It also provides a datum point for considering any future development of your talents outside of the normal educational process. An indication will also be gained of directions in which you may have any special gifts or aptitudes. Motivation, enthusiasm, ability to rise above disappointments, relationships with others, a broadening or narrowing of interests – information about all of these subjects may come from questions asked under this heading.

■ ***Further or higher education***

This is a continuation of the previous area for those who have had the opportunity to experience it and provides further information on the characteristics and attributes already mentioned. It is yet another transition in life which can bring more trauma to some people than others: some people cope better than others with what is often their first taste of independence.

For people who have had the benefit of further or higher education, consider the reasons for your choice of studies, what options of subject, colleges and why, how final selection was made, coping with transitions from secondary to tertiary education, subjects taken year by year with results and why, practical projects undertaken, how were projects selected, managed and supervised, how relevant to occupational needs, social life at college, participation in community life, time out, re-sits, work experience during term and vacations, relationships with academic and non-academic staff, other students, development of personal characteristics, personal and social learning as well as academic, final results achieved compared with expectations. Finally, reflect on the value of what you did from academic, occupational, personal and social points of view.

A typical starter could be:

'Tell me about your time at college/university.'
Your response should be a rapid tour through what you did, your reasons for doing it and the impact it made upon you as a person. A more negative approach by an interviewer might be:

'Your results look somewhat disappointing!'
Against whom or what might they be comparing you? Your early promise, what your peers might have done, some absolute standard because you only passed instead of getting better grades or final results? Perhaps you too were disappointed? Was there a reason – and to what extent was it because of you? Or are you going to blame someone else? Perhaps you did better than you originally thought? If you could have done better, what lessons(s) did you learn which you have since put into practice? Prepare for this one and have a respectable reply ready. Other questions may cover such topics as:

How were your studies financed?
What did you do during vacations?
What were your choices of college?

What subjects did you study?
Who or what influenced you to study your chosen subjects?
What offices or responsibilities did you hold?
Did you receive any special honours or awards?
What did you get up to outside of your academic studies?
What did you do to increase your income whilst studying?
What practical projects did you undertake?
How successful were your projects?
How were your projects decided upon?
How were they managed and supervised?
What were the most difficult things about your projects?
Were you doing your projects by yourself or with others?
How did your results compare with what you expected to achieve?
What were the reactions of your tutors, colleagues and family to your results?
Looking back, what were the subjects you really enjoyed most/least?
What was the most outstanding memory you have of this period of your life?
Do you feel you could have done better at anything and if so, how?
What did you learn about yourself as a person during this time?
When did you start think about what to do when you finished your studies?
Which career directions did you narrow down to and why those particular choices?
If you could change anything about your higher education, what would it be?
Looking back, what were the greatest influences on your life at college?

Remember – qualifications are often a bonus for the employer and not a prerequisite. What they do is 'add interview weight' – they help you to get there but don't normally guarantee your success.

Motivation, self-discipline, organizing ability, persuasiveness, concern for others, widening of social awareness, inter-personal skills, range of interests, ability to cope under pressure, enthusiasm, competitiveness, comparison against peers, strength and direction of career aspirations, need for various degrees of independence or dependence may all be inferred from the answers to these and similar questions.

■ ***Occupational training and work experiences***

This usually represents the largest single, continuous period in your life. It provides you with your status, satisfaction, power and standard of living. It is the culmination of the preceding years – and usually the reason why an organization wants to employ you.

If you are a young person you should be able to talk very freely about the facts and feelings relating to your first work experiences such as a Saturday job, delivery rounds, holiday/vacation jobs, likes/dislikes, personal growth, financial and social benefits.

Then you may have to recall formal occupational training experiences: how chosen, what, why, how long, subjects studied, skills acquired, level of competence, certification, likes/dislikes/preferences, value of experiences, relations with staff and students, extra-mural activities, key learning experiences, value in working situations, etc.

Regardless of your age, for each job you have held, but particularly for those, say, in the last ten years, you should review and be prepared to talk about these aspects: how did you get the job, why you chose that job or company, influence of others (parents/relatives) on choice, method of selection, induction and training given, job responsibilities, what was achieved or contributed in measurable terms, financial aspects such as level of spending, budgeting, monitoring expenditure, numbers supervised or managed, salary progression, promotions/moves, assignments, appointments/experiences overseas, introducing changes in procedures, systems, technology, cost savings, innovation, highlights/low points, personal achievements/contributions of merit, job likes and dislikes, motivators/demotivators, changes you would have made if allowed to do so, relations with others in all directions at all levels, reasons for seeking a move, personal and occupational career growth in each job, most difficult problem overcome and how, most annoying aspect of work, effects of work on personal, social and family life, rewards and compensations obtained and sought, description of ideal job in 'x' years' time.

If your work experiences are purely part-time, Saturday jobs or during vacations, then demonstrate how your experience is related to their job. Explain what you contributed and learned. For undergraduates this is often their first opportunity to mix with 'real' people of different ages and backgrounds working for a living and who are not students. For other young people it can demonstrate levels of interest and motivation. Some of the most common ways to start you talking about this area of your life are:

'Tell me about your present/last job/vacation work.'
If you can't talk easily and answer questions about your jobs, what can you do? Your responses should especially concentrate upon those parts of your work history which mirror what the organization is seeking. Make your reply succinct, articulate and jargon-free. Always talk about your achievements, contributions, what you have learned – especially in relation to their job. This could lead on to:

'What do you think of your present/last employer?'
Don't bite the hand that fed/feeds you. Emphasize the good things that you learned and contributed. If pressed for something negative, look at what the new job offers, which presumably is missing in the last/present appointment? Another hardy annual is:

'Why change jobs?'
You may have a genuine reason – no prospects, organization is slow to change, you aren't using your talents fully, technological or systems changes have reduced job satisfaction and prospects, reduced opportunity to learn and grow. Whatever it is, you might have to answer supplementary questions. When planning your reply, avoid putting down your present or last employer and don't say anything that could reflect negatively on you, such as being bored, or feeling it is just time for a change for no obvious reason(s). It is much more appropriate to look at what they are offering and say that their work would seem to give you scope to make a useful contribution and for personal growth (in that order - what they get first and what you get second!). Classic, predictable, follow-up questions include:

'What makes you think you'll be able to do our job?'
'Why do you want to work for us/change jobs?'
'What interests you about this appointment?'
'Why should we employ you?'

You should make brief, pointed comparisons between the job description and personnel specification as you understand them and your ability to fulfil their needs. Quickly summarise what you have to offer in terms of job content and personal characteristics – appropriate experiences, enthusiasm, interest, motivation, challenge, etc. Don't ramble on too long! Be prepared to back up any of your assertions. This is the perfect question on which to use the results of your job matching exercise from Chapter 4 (see p. 84). It would be unusual if the interviewer didn't want to know:

'What tangible contribution are you making in your present job?'
This is increasingly predictable – even when you feel your work is one of the 'not measurable' kind. So how do you really earn your keep and add value to your organization? What do they pay you to achieve? Think about your achievements and be prepared to put them across. The closer your present contributions are to what this organization is looking for, the better you will come across. The follow-up is likely to be:

'And how long do you think it will be before you are making a contribution in this job?'
Think about an acceptable reply in relation to their job and company culture. Are they taking an unprecedented leap into the twentieth century or actually preparing themselves for the twenty-first? Comment on what you need to 'pick up' to understand the job context and content before you can contribute. Try to be realistic. Some typically provocative questions might include:

'I don't think you have the right experience for this job!'
'You're not the right person for this job!'
Try not to answer these questions as stated. Turn them around and emphasize the things you can do and the qualities you do have rather than defend yourself. Be positive about what you can do and never say what you can't do or to make negative judgements about yourself or your experiences. Put over the view that you are a quick learner and believe that the gaps between yourself and their ideal candidate would soon be rectified.

Avoid slipping into the trap of getting the interviewers to justify what they have said. The discussion could become adversarial – they highlight your deficiencies and, in doing so, reinforce their feelings against you. By this point in the interview you might genuinely agree that this is not the job for you. You may wish to say so and even be able to move on to ask whether or not there are/will be any appointments within the organization for which you could be more suitable.

A wide variety of questions could arise under this heading:

Why is there a gap in your CV?
How did you go about getting your first job?
What was it which attracted you to that job or company?
What were you employed as?
What has your salary progression been?
What training did they give you?
Were you ever required to dismiss anyone?
Why and how did you go about it?
What were your responsibilities?
How well did you get on in that job?
What responsibility did you have for setting objectives for yourself or others?
What sort of planning did you have to do?
Do you have any special way of making decisions?
What tactics do you use to motivate people?
Which parts of the work did you like most?
What was your last boss's greatest weakness/strength?
What's your favourite way of communicating with people?
What were the least attractive aspects of that job?
If you had to deal with either managing directors or trainees, which would you choose?
What prospects have you in your present job?
What sort of people do you supervise/manage?
Did you get any promotions? Why and how?
What difficulties did you have in talking to poorer performers?
How would you describe your style of supervising/managing?
What financial responsibilities did you have?
How do you go about problem-solving?
What was the toughest problem you had to deal with and what happened?
If you could make some changes in your job, what would they be?
Looking back, what did you feel were your greatest contributions to that job?
Considering all your jobs and employers, which was the most satisfactory and why?
What have been your greatest contributions in any job?
If you were going to start again, what changes would you make?

Interviewers often concentrate on this area to the exclusion of others. From your answers they will make a large number of important assumptions – which sometimes they will neither tell you about nor test in any other way. Your work experiences can provide evidence of interest, motivation, interpersonal skills, persistence, use of intellect, ambitions, job satisfaction, depth and range of abilities and aptitudes, forethought, organising, planning and problem-solving skills, creativity, ability to withstand stress and pressure, ability to get work done by others, supervisory skills, desire or otherwise to cooperate, commitment to work – a vast range of attributes.

- ***Life and interests outside school and work***

When you go to work you agree to undertake certain activities, fulfil obligations and receive certain rewards and benefits: there is a contract of exchange. Your life is to a greater or lesser degree controlled by the organization. But what do you choose to do with your life when you are in charge of it – away from work? Thoughtful interviewers realise that it is vital to explore your activities away from work for two main reasons. Firstly they might throw light on the extent to which your outside activities support or militate against good job performance. And secondly – even more important – because of the many clues they give about you as an individual.

You ought to brush up the facts and feelings about the development of your leisure pursuits and hobbies/interests from earliest days, what and why, whether still pursued, developments with age, current interests, depth of involvement, effects on social and working life, benefits and satisfactions gained from pursuits, what has been given up/sacrificed to maintain interests, local/national/international acknowledgement of your expertise, work in community, social, religious, professional activities, what, why, where, how often. Interviewers will ask you about the strength and direction of your interests and your chosen ways of relaxing. A typical starter is:

'Tell me what you do in your spare time.'
Quickly go over your outside activities – perhaps going back some years if they are still relevant. It might be better to start with the current situation and say how these may have changed over the years. But you could always use a chronological approach.

Describe your depth of involvement and breadth of interests. Highlight possible relevance to the job and the organization. Give examples of satisfaction obtained and the reasons for originally pursuing them. Get the balance right between personal development, relaxation and the need to be committed to working for the organization. You may have an unusual outside interest and they may pick on that one to start with. Don't fall into the common trap of giving the impression that you do just about everything going – and then can't answer a single question on any of the things you have written on your application. The interviewers may be concerned about any adverse impact of your interests on the job for which you are being interviewed:

'It seems to me that you might have difficulty in maintaining that interest because of the nature of our job.'
'How will that activity fit in with our job?'
These are ones which you can predict. Maybe you can turn them around and ask: 'How do you mean?' or 'Had you any specific things in mind?' – in as nice a way as possible. This might allow you to allay any fears they may have. Indicate how you fit them in to your life and work at present. Perhaps the interviewer is correct and you are being faced with a choice: will you have to adapt your interests to the job or decide the work is not for you? What is your answer going to be? The usual questions asked under this particular heading include:

How do you relax and unwind?
What sort of books do you read?
Tell me about the last book you read.
What holidays do you get at present?
What TV programmes do you like/watch?
How much time do these interests take up?
Have you any positions of responsibility outside of work?
What about activities related to the community, social service, working with and helping others or religious interests?
If you could only pursue one of your current interests, which would it be?
In what ways might your outside interests be of use in doing this job?
What difficulties can you foresee in pursuing your interests and doing the work we have in mind?

From this they will infer such things as your motivation, opportunity to organize others, plan, exercise control, solve problems, creativity and communication skills. Your outside interests may also be a compensation for less satisfying aspects of work. They become opportunities to develop and use valued skills and abilities which are under-utilised at work. They will also influence your desire and ability to do the job, impose constraints which might impinge on your work responsibilities, develop skills which could be of value at work, provide opportunities for life and career changes, build interpersonal skills and indicate personal value systems. In other words, looking at this part of your life helps them to build up a more rounded picture of you as an individual than that which is obtained merely by exploring your working life.

- ***Your present circumstances***

This brings the interviewer up to date and provides information for assessing what has happened to you from your earliest days: what you have done with your life and where you are now. Your present situation may help or hinder you in carrying out the job they have in mind: the location, hours, rewards, inconveniences which may militate against you accepting or settling in and making a contribution. An easy opener might be:

'Tell me about your present domestic/family situation.'
Cover the sort of things mentioned above – location, family, mobility. Be prepared for follow-up questions about the likely effects of any of these on your job performance. If they know you have been divorced, separated or remarried, then they may be probing this in a roundabout way. It may be easy to set their minds at rest – even though you might consider this to be prying into your private life and even close to discrimination. If you do not satisfy their curiosity, they may make unjustifiable inferences from a position of ignorance. You may be rejected as a 'bad bet' because they have a feeling that your situation may interfere with job performance.

In the prevailing economic climate this is another predictable question:

'Why have you been unemployed so long?'
It is not uncommon now to have had some period(s) of

unemployment. These might have been due to a number of reasons. Such a question should not worry you if you have been doing something productive whilst unemployed. Talk to the interviewer in terms of:

How your unemployment came about
Your job hunting tactics
Any community or 'free' work you have been doing
Ways in which you have maintained the market value of your major asset – your property
What training or learning experiences you have had

Try to be positive and show that you have not let the grass grow under your feet. The interviewer will be more impressed if you have been doing something than if you have not. Other questions under this area include:

What family commitments do you have?
Do you take work home each day or at weekends?
How do you get to and from work at present?
What happens when that method doesn't work?
How will your partner/family react if you get this job?
How does your partner/family feel about all of your travelling?
What would you do about relocating if offered this appointment?
What effects would taking this appointment have on your present family situation?

This is an area which a competent interviewer must explore. It provides clues about your balance between work and home – your motivation, aspirations, ability to cope with the demands of the job and your family and domestic responsibilities.

■ ***You as an individual***

Let me suggest that, as people rise up within organizations, they are more likely to fail not because of technical incompetence, but because of a lack of ability to relate to other people and get things done using their interpersonal skills. If there is any truth in this idea, then one of the most important aspects the interviewers will be trying to find out is 'what makes you tick' and how you relate to other people. For some jobs it is going to be the make-or-break factor. In other jobs they can employ a loner who will produce excellent results working independently or with the minimum of human contact.

Your preparation consists of thinking how you would you describe yourself as a person in terms of your strongest or most outstanding traits and characteristics, i.e. what motivates you, what has given you greatest satisfaction/dissatisfaction in life, how you have changed, what would you change if given the chance to make different decisions about anything, what annoys you most, how you have coped with disappointments, what have been your greatest work and non-work achievements.

Interviewers make a large number of conclusions about your personality traits and characteristics from asking both indirect and direct questions. Some of the direct ones are rather obvious, e.g. 'What sort of person are you?'. It is often difficult to know what intellectual leaps they make from an indirect question to you possessing some trait or not. A much-used question under this heading is:

'When was the last time you worked under pressure and how did you cope?'
Think of your example. Explain how it arose and how you dealt with it. Is the interviewer asking because this job is stressful? Perhaps you could start a dialogue on the job content and relate your ability to work under pressure to their needs. Other examples are:

What do you feel is your greatest weakness?
What do you think of your present/last boss?
What sort of thing gets you annoyed and frustrated?
Which department seems to give you the most trouble?
How well do you get on with your boss/colleagues/staff?
Tell me about the last time you had to get rid of someone.
You certainly seem to have had a lot of job moves. Why?
How much socializing do you have to do in your present job?
What would you say is the best way of getting good results out of you?
Tell me about the most difficult person you have had to deal with.
If we took up references from your present employers, what would they say about you?

There can't be many people who have not worked with difficult co-workers, been overloaded with work from time to time, have had disagreements with someone or some department, have some weaknesses, etc. Do you really believe that everyone around you thinks you're great all of the time? Is it possible to work in any organization where resources are scarce and not come up against someone who is competing for the same resources? Think about these for yourself and work up example answers which do not leave a bad taste with the interviewer. You're not human if you haven't made a mistake – and some people would say if you haven't made a mistake then you probably haven't taken a risk or achieved very much at all!

Don't say anything negative about yourself unless you are able to finish off your reply by showing how you have learned and prospered from the experience. Faults should not be large or irreversible. Try to think about your 'allowable weaknesses'. Disagreements must be shown to have been resolved and left a reasonable working relationship behind. If you've sacked someone, then relate the facts and your feelings. Here are some more questions under this heading:

What makes you laugh?
Can you suffer fools gladly?
How would you describe yourself?
What sort of things frustrate you?
What are your strongest characteristics?
What makes you angry and how do you deal with it?
In what ways have you sometimes let yourself down?
What sort of things have made you take time off work?
If you could re-live a period in the past, when would it be?
If you could change something in your life, what would it be?
Which single personal skill would you like to improve or acquire?
What have you got to keep under tight control when dealing with some people?
If you were to give some advice about life to your children, what would it be?

The type of characteristics in which they might be interested and which would come out of questions asked under this area include sociability, perseverance, ability to cope with stress and work under pressure, leadership, maturity, forethought, application, integrity, energy, stability, honesty, etc. Organizations are increasingly using psychological questionnaires to provide independent and objective information on various traits to supplement the assessments made during interviews.

■ ***You, this job and the future***

Naturally the interviewers will want to know not only whether you can do the job but also how much you want to do it. Is it a career step or simply a ploy to get better terms out of your present employer? Is it a safe port in a storm or something you really think is worthwhile? Questions such as these reflect the interviewers' interest in this area:

'What interests you most about this work?
'Why do you think we should give you this job?'
'Summarize why you are the best candidate for this appointment.'
These are golden opportunities for you to leave a good impression in the minds of the interviewers. 'Well, as I understand it, you are looking for someone to . . . and my experience as/with . . . is of this type. I feel that I am able to bring . . . to the job and see the work as an opportunity to use some of the things I like doing and to extend my experiences . . .'

'What changes do you think you might make if you joined us?'
You must seriously think of how you are going to respond to this standard question. Beware of saying you are going to change the world when you join them – you may be burying the brainchild of one of the interviewers. This one may be predictable from the prior information you get about the job. Possibly it may only be answered in the light of further information gleaned during the interview. How about: 'Well, there are some things which I would want to have a look at such as . . . to see whether or not they could be 'fine-tuned'.

Here are examples of another hardy annual topic which comes in a variety of forms and is one you must also think about – the future. It indicates not only your values, motivation and ambitions, but also your ideas of reality and what practical steps you are taking to make it come true.

'Where do you see yourself in 'x' years time?'
'What would you like to be doing in 'x' years time?'
It is an omission on a grand scale if you have not thought about this question and how you propose to answer it. 'I should like to be . . . in about 'x' years time and what I am doing towards this is . . .' Some indication of your direction of interest, ability to plan

and move consistently towards goals will be inferred from this type of conversation. How real the desire is, or the extent to which the organization may be able to accommodate your aspirations is also very important for them to discover.

'Would you like to have your boss's job?'
Well, would you? If yes, why? If not, why not? Will your replies in either case hold water and be acceptable? Think about why an interviewer might ask you this – is it because you seem over-ambitious or have you expressed some negative views about your boss? Or is the questioner testing you to see what would happen:

'If we invite you to join us, you hand in your notice and your present company offer you more money or a promotion, what would you do?'
Another predictable one if you have given the impression of being the type of person who is only concerned about 'the main chance' and have expressed regrets with the way you have been treated by your present employer. Or perhaps you have not been very positive about your reasons for wanting to change jobs. What would you really do? Is it a possibility? Are your present employers like that? Are you really only trying to get another job offer to put your present boss on the spot? If you want to stand a chance at being considered for the new job, then you must take this as an opportunity to reiterate the benefits of moving rather than of staying – perhaps in the mid-term or long run as opposed to the immediate future. If you are really looking for personal growth and development which your present employer can't offer, then you must find the right words to support your desire to move.

Other questions which may arise under this area include:

You are too good for this work!
Have you ever used our services?
How would you dress for this job?
Tell me something about our company?
What do you know about our products?
How did you come to apply for this job?
What retirement plans do you have?
How do you feel about pension schemes?
How long do you think you'll stay with us?
Does working overseas attract you?
What sort of salary/package are you looking for?

What is the greatest barrier to you accepting an offer if we made one?

■ ***Miscellaneous***

There are dozens of other questions which might be classified under one of the above categories or this heading such as:

'You seem to be a bit of a job-hopper.'
You just have to predict this one if you have 'moved around' a bit. No excuses for not being able to rationalize your career moves in retrospect. There are a number of reasons for moving – talk about them, but remember, no 'biting the hand . . .'. Do the facts support your reasons? Was it just for money and your application form confirms this? Don't get irritable or become defensive. The fit between some people and where they work is far from perfect. Be careful that the things you have been moving away from are not present in this organization and that the things you want to move towards are.

'Have you ever been dismissed?'
Unexplained gaps in your application might bring out this question. This is another predictable request so you must have a good explanation. Remember, the most useful purpose of using references as part of an assessment procedure is to check information obtained from other sources such as application forms and during interviews. Work out supportable reasons which will 'pass muster'! And don't become bitter and twisted about the event. Show you have taken it in your stride, benefitted from it and it is now behind you. Here is a selection of questions which might appear under this 'catch-all' heading:

What other job offers have you got at present?
Have you always had a beard/moustache, etc?
Do you normally dress like that for an interview?
What's the most worrying thing in the news today?
What mistakes have you made in the past five years?
What will you have most difficulty dealing with?
How will your mobility affect your job performance?
If we were to offer you this job, would you take it?
Try to sell me this pen/watch/calculator/Ansaphone.
If you could design your ideal job, what would it be?

How do you feel about taking a psychological test now?
What would you most like to change in the world today?
What sort of training would you need to do this job well?
We have a non-smoking policy. How will that affect you?
What has been the most difficult time financially for you?
How would you go about doing your boss's job if you got it?
Under what circumstances do you cooperate best with others?
What has been the most challenging thing you have ever done?
What are you looking for – job satisfaction or a high salary?
If you could only have one, which would it be?
If you were to offer advice to an interviewer, what would it be?
How do you feel about everyone else being younger/older than you?
What past events would you want to avoid recurring in the future?
If we offered you a job subject to probation, what would you say?
If we paid your removal expenses and you left within a couple of years, would you pay us back?
If your boss asks you to do something you don't like or disagree with, what do you do?
You do realize that there will be no chance of promotion in this job?
Have you ever been passed over for promotion or failed a Board?
Why, and what did you do about it?
What do you think you are bringing to the job we don't already have?
You will have to work with outside consultants in this job. What are your reactions to that?
If you had another offer alongside ours, which one would you choose?
Have you any activities outside work which bring in extra money?

You see what I mean – there is no end to it! Many of these questions are probably not too difficult to respond to, even on the spot. It could be the follow-up questions arising out of your first answer which are more difficult. You are usually going to be asked to clarify, justify or defend what you say. Interviewers cannot prepare for every eventuality and neither can you. They have to prepare for all the candidates; you only have to do it for yourself. In general terms, what you should be seeking to do in reply to their questions is to provide *socially acceptable responses!*

Interviewers' questioning techniques

Most interviewers wish to control the discussion so that they can cover the areas which are important to them. They will do this in a number of ways. Initially they might set the scene and tell you the role they wish you to play:

'I will ask questions about you, your background and work experience and your interests outside work, then later I shall be pleased to answer any of your questions about the job and the company . . .'

Others will produce checklists of the introductory remarks and areas to cover, forewarning you when they wish to move from topic to topic, using 'briefly' or 'brief' when asking you to respond to some questions, making statements or using phrases such as 'Can I ask you to move on . . .', 'Could we now move on to . . .' They will also look at their watches and their checklists from time to time.

However, the most powerful ways of control are through their use of different questioning techniques and their body language. The form their questions take influences your responses, the information they obtain and the inferences and final judgements they make. Some questions are going to be 'better' than others. Some questioners are going to be more skilled, but in some interviews you are going to have to work hard to make a good impression because of the poor questioning techniques.

There are a number of types of questions, statements and techniques common to all interviews. They vary in their degree of structure, from open or broad at one end, through probing, technical or 'test', hypothetical, multiple or forced choice, summarising/reflecting-back and leading to closed questions at the other extreme.

■ *Open questions*

These are intended to get you talking without prescribing the direction of the conversation too tightly. You cannot give a yes or no answer and have to respond in your own words. Often you will reply not only with facts but with feelings and attitudes. It is a useful way for the interviewer to get you to explore topics or expand on your feelings. The classic approach is not really a question but a request:

'Tell me about . . .'
This gives you a very free hand and you should use it to present yourself in as attractive a way as possible. Another less structured question is:

'How do you feel about . . .?'
Other examples include:

'Describe how you organized yourself to complete that project.'
'What sort of things do you feel have been of value?'
'Which other technical areas are of interest to you?'
'What sort of supervision do you think brings out the best in people?'

- ***Probing questions***

Often questions starting with 'W' are probes, such as:

'What was your reason for saying that?'
'Who else was involved in that project?'
'Why does that seem to worry you?'
'When did you recognize that you wanted to change career direction?'
'Where do you think you could get those materials from in addition to your present supplier?'

And there are questions beginning with 'How':

'How did you resolve that problem?'
'How did you react to . . . ?
'How did that affect the outcome of . . . ?

The probe is aimed at obtaining more information, clarifying or getting you to justify what you have just said. It may also be used if you are drifting away from the point or just talking too much. They tend to be quite specific, some of which ought to be predictable when you are doing your preparation, but many will arise from your last response.

- ***Test or technical questions***

Another type of question are those specifically related to the technical aspects of the work such as:

'Describe the way in which . . . works.'
'How would you go about solving this type of problem?'
'If . . . happened, what would you do about it?'

'Explain what is meant by . . .'
'If you got this result . . . , what would you think is causing it?'
'What do you understand by . . . ?'
'Give me an example of . . .'

These are usually asking you to talk about work experiences which ought to be fresh in your memory. In interviews where you have been provided with a job description, you should have 'guess-timated' some of the likely technical questions implicit in the job responsibilities.

- ***Hypothetical questions***

These questions place you into a 'What if . . .' situation to see how you might respond:

'What would you do if you were confronted by a very irate customer?'
'What would you do if an employees' representative came to you and said that unless you were prepared to re-instate a particular employee he would call his members out on strike?'
'Tell me how you would go about organizing a pop concert.'
'What would you do if . . . ?'

Interviewers may have a number of reasons for asking hypothetical questions. It may be an actual situation which you have to face. It could be an awkward question they have had to answer themselves which has become part of their repertoire or perhaps it is to test your ability to think quickly in strange situations. Whatever their motives, you should treat it as a serious request and answer it to the best of your ability. They might be prepared to answer one or two questions from you to put their question into a particular context, but they may throw it straight back at you to answer as soon as possible.

- ***Multiple questions***

These questions can be confusing. Which part do you tackle first?

'Perhaps you would tell me about your early school days and I'd also like to know about what you do outside work and which parts of your job you find most frustrating.'

It could just be a poorly-trained interviewer or someone who believes they are testing your memory. It certainly could feel like a

Catch-22 situation. You may well reply by asking: 'Have you any particular preference which one I should answer first?' Better still, try 'Let me tell you about . . . and then move on to . . . and finish with some comments on . . .' You should always consider this type of multiple question as an opportunity to sell some aspect of yourself in relation to the job which may not have been broached up to that time.

- ***Forced choice questions***

There may be occasions when you will be tested or challenged by questions such as:

'If you were confronted with two equally able candidates for a job and one was older than the other, which would you choose and why?'
'Do you think it is better to provide managers with company vehicles, hire vehicles, increase their salary to allow them to buy their own or give them a car user's allowance which would help them to run their own vehicle at company expense?'
'When you were working for that company, did you use external consultants, do it yourself or establish an in-company task force?'

Once again the questioners could have many and varied motives for asking these. The options may be the interviewers' 'pet' solutions which have been tried or problems the organization has had to face. You do not necessarily have to agree with the options. Perhaps you wish to provide alternatives which you have used? You may be able to ask questions for clarification – but often interviewers don't like being interviewed themselves. They believe they are in charge and want you to provide answers, not ask questions. One way of overcoming this possible objection is to slip into a rhetorical mode. Ask your questions aloud and answer them for yourself: 'Well, it would all depend on what timescale I was working against and how much cash was available. If I assume that it had to be completed as soon as possible with a limited budget, then probably the better option would be to . . .', etc.

- ***Summarising questions***

This allows them to confirm what you have said:

'So what you are saying is . . .?'
'Let me see if I understand what you do in your present job.'

You can also use this technique yourself – especially if you have been asked about something novel or complex and wish to check out the question before trying to answer it.

- ***Reflecting-back***

The interviewer may use this technique just to keep you talking without making and judgements on what you are saying:

'I've never come across that technique before.'
'So multiple regression analysis is new to you?'

The interviewer is probably expecting you to expand on your lack of familiarity with the technique – possibly by asking some sensible questions about what it is, when it is used, how difficult it might be to learn, etc.

- ***Leading questions***

These are questions which might tell you what interviewers are thinking – and that they may even wish you to confirm their prejudices. Some interviewers use them in an adversarial manner – they wish you to disagree and support your disagreement. Typical approaches are:

'I think . . . , what do you think?'
'You don't think . . . , do you?'
'Isn't it quite dreadful the way . . . nowadays?'
'I suppose you feel . . . is acceptable?'
'I wouldn't want to try . . . , how about you?'
'You can work under pressure, can't you?'
'I guess that working long irregular hours is OK with you?'
'A lot of travelling wouldn't worry you, would it?'

Often the interviewers will be 'giving away' the answer they want to hear, perhaps they are projecting their own feelings. They may also be telling you – unwittingly or otherwise – of what the work entails and suggesting that you should conform to the organization's requirements. They may also be trying to get you to admit to something or just finding out your views on something. The problem with this 'game' is that you don't know whether they want you to agree (because they feel their point of view is important) or they want to stir you up to put the opposite point of view and defend it. The choice is yours. If you feel strongly about something, which happens to be the opposite to what they are saying, perhaps you should put across your ideas in a logical and rational way? Try not to take the bait and respond emotionally. You may ask them if that is the organization's stance in such circumstances. Their reply may start to persuade you that perhaps this is not the company you would wish to work for.

- ***Closed questions***

These are ones which are framed in such a way that you can theoretically reply with a 'Yes' or a 'No'. This technique is often used by what I call the 'Icy Interviewers':

'I see you went to . . .'
'I see you have . . .'
'I see you like . . .'
'I see you worked for . . .'

And so they go on . . . reading from your CV or application form, learning nothing new, confirming that they can read and you can hear. And there are the other classics:

'Did you like . . . ?'
'Did you feel you had reached a dead end in that job?'
'Have your frequent changes been due to boredom?'
'I suppose you enjoy good health?'

Faced with this type of person and sort of questioning, you should not fall into the trap of saying only 'Yes' or 'No'. Take the opportunity to sell yourself. Elaborate your answers. Say 'Yes, and I . . .' or 'No, but I . . .'. Offer more information, volunteer facts and opinions.

Be wary of the interviewer who uses the 'playing dumb' tactic:

'I'm not an expert, but could you . . .?'

This person may not be an expert and is testing to see whether or not you are able to communicate your ideas in a way which would be understandable to laymen. Perhaps that's an important part of the job? However, they may well be experts and they are really testing your knowledge of what you are saying or how you might apply your specialist knowledge.

Whichever of the above techniques is used, you must try to optimize the situation and communicate as many positive and relevant facts about yourself. This might mean adding to the questions as well as giving them what they want. Sometimes you have to think quickly to yourself: 'What is this person really getting at?'. Without becoming paranoid about some complex underlying motivation, try to be as forthcoming as you can. If you have concerns, then find a suitable way of expressing them. You could always try a reflecting-back technique in which you check out your fears/suspicions/understanding by saying: 'Are you really concerned about/saying that . . .?'

If you haven't understood a question, ask for it to be repeated or restate what you think has been asked to check if your understanding is correct. If you have only a passing acquaintance with a topic, say so and thus qualify your answer before you give it. This provides a datum point against which the interviewer can judge your reply.

Whatever happens, don't try to bluff your way through the interview. It is relatively easy for skilled interviewers to push you into an intellectual corner. They always know more about their organization than you do. You may be an expert or have lengthy experience in an activity where the interviewer is less knowledgeable. Be wary of talking down to interviewers or denigrating them in any way whatsoever. You should always be prepared to disclose something interesting about yourself which they have not requested. But it must be something related to the job and must be something positive about yourself and your work experiences.

By following the guidelines in this chapter, you should be able to produce a brief, attractive, articulate, spoken summary of yourself under any of the questioning areas and without too much trouble. You should know your strengths and show how you would use them if you were appointed. You should also know your weaknesses and how these can be overcome or avoided when necessary. Above all, you must be able to talk fluently about all of your jobs in the terms outlined here. There is no one else who can do any of this for you! You cannot engage an advocate on your behalf. No one can make your case to the interviewer as attractively and comprehensively as you can, provided you *take the trouble to prepare yourself!*

3 How can I make a good impression?

'Everyone lives by selling something.'

Across The Plains
Robert Louis Stevenson

This chapter is about communication, starting by looking at ways in which you communicate symbolically through your appearance. Then you can complete and analyse an exercise related to your interaction with other people. Your ways of using words and how you communicate through your body language are considered next. Finally, we look at your listening skills.

Symbolic communication - your appearance

One of the factors upon which many interviewers place undue emphasis is your initial impact. This is gained largely through what you are 'saying' to people symbolically through your clothing, hair, jewellery and cosmetics. What interviewers may infer about you from these could range from: 'This person is not worried about what we think of them' through to 'They feel that their appearance is important for this job and have taken some care with it just for us.' Let's have a look at these symbolic ways of communicating.

■ *Clothing*

How you dress reveals a great deal about your self-image, your values and attitudes towards other people and situations. Differences in occupational status are associated with what is worn: the 'city' type wearing a suit, the manual worker in some form of overall, people in service jobs wearing a company uniform. For interviews it is wise to find out what is expected or acceptable within the culture you are trying to enter. A preliminary visit might help. You may have a picture from your experience of what the people wear in the organization. What might be acceptable in an artistic media setting will probably be different from that expected of you in a multi-national company or a high street bank. Some cultures, such as academia, are probably more liberal and would not be thrown if you appeared looking like the stereotype of the intellectual. Usually the academic interviewer's interest will be in the extent to which your intellectual eminence and research work will bring fame and fortune to their establishment and it is unlikely that personal appearance will rank highly amongst the critical requirements for successful job performance.

Irrespective of sex, something fairly conservative would be a good choice. Interviewers expect you to be reasonably well turned out and will only notice if you are not!

For men, it would usually be safe to wear a lounge suit or sports jacket and trousers. Sweat-shirts, jeans and trainers may be acceptable for some jobs or preliminary 'chats' with some organizations – but you'd have to be really sure before turning up dressed like that. A phone call to the organization beforehand would be worthwhile. The old leg-pull about 'Wearing the interview suit, I see' is not too far from the truth. You should probably have something which serves this purpose.

Women should probably wear a business suit. A skirt and blouse with jacket in neutral colours with a slight contrast to relieve the overall appearance could be a reasonable alternative. Trouser suits and culottes are a possibility – but think and enquire before making your final decision. Summer dresses may just be allowable, but you should probably avoid anything too casual for a business environment. Once again, these may be quite acceptable for working in some retail outlets – but not at a supervisory or managerial level. It would probably be better not to attract too much attention by over-short skirts or rather low-cut tops – try not to distract! One small piece of research on the effect of what women wore and the assessments made by interviewers suggested that the more masculine the candidate's dress, the higher the assessment made by the interviewers!

If you have bought a special interview outfit, accessories or shoes, etc, it is wise to ensure that they are comfortable before you wear them for the interview. There can be nothing more uncomfortable and distracting than shoes that pinch, a shirt that rubs at the neck or the stiffness often found in new clothes. You should also think about the condition and appearance of your footwear. A pair of clean and polished shoes may not be particularly noticed; a pair of dirty, down-at-heel ones will.

Don't forget overall cleanliness, condition of your hands and nails and the like. They won't be noticed if they are OK – only if they are not.

If you are staying away overnight as part of your selection procedure, take an extra suit, shirt, blouse, tie, socks, tights, etc. Some of these are useful even if you are only going along for an interview. You must have heard some of the horror stories of what has happened to some unfortunate candidates on the way to an interview by car or public transport. And, of course, things could still happen to you when you arrive and are having meals or refreshments. All these normally innocent situations can become potentially hazardous events which can blemish your clothing and do little for your appearance and self-confidence. Interviewers may well allow for such things happening, but it is better to be safe than sorry.

In general terms you should aim to look smart – (dry) cleaned, ironed and without 'canteen medals' on lapels, ties or blouses. Strangers (interviewers) will relate more easily to you if you appear smart and this can only be to your benefit at the outset of your interview. Smartly dressed people are often attributed with more favourable qualities. Attractive people are probably treated better, have more satisfying and rewarding encounters and develop greater social skills. Beauty probably is more than skin deep and a reasonable outward appearance certainly helps. Buy something new and wear it, even if it is only a small, inexpensive item. Make yourself feel good outside and you'll feel good inside.

The overall message is 'moderation in all things' if you don't want to be remembered for the wrong reasons. If you want to be a memorable candidate for the wrong reasons, go to the extremes. You might give the interviewers something to discuss but it won't be about sending you a job offer!

■ *Hair*

The way you wear your hair will be interpreted in different ways from 'rebel' through to 'strict conformist'. It says something about you – although exactly what it says and what will be deduced by the interviewers is not quite clear. There are plenty of prejudices about people with hair of different styles and lengths. Think about men with crew cuts, pony tails or shoulder length hair. Are men with long hair effeminate and women with cropped hair macho? As a woman, you may even have to be careful about not having a more expensive coiffeur than the interviewers could afford. There is no excuse for turning up with a bird's nest on top of or surrounding the face – although the stereotype of some academics might create the right impression for some appointments. Men with dark beards should check their overall appearance in the mirror before finally choosing which suit to wear. A dark beard and a dark suit can create a strange impression when there is a little, round face poking out of it.

Facial hair on men or women can raise eyebrows. On men it is often associated with academic, rebellious or artistic inclinations. For women, it can be thought to suggest masculinity! There are still some occupations and organizations where men with beards will face some opposition during the interview – and may even be asked if they would be prepared to become clean-shaven if offered employment. As for styles? If you are going into fashion, hair styling or the beauty business, then you should have some idea of what is expected and acceptable.

For both sexes, the most important thing to say about hair is that it should be clean, tidy, neat – and brushed or combed just before you go into the interview! Otherwise keep away from extremes.

■ ***Jewellery***

Wearing jewellery is no longer the preserve of women. Younger men with earrings are now more common. But there will still be interviewers who attribute unacceptable characteristics to men wearing them. You could always think about removing them when going for an interview with a particular type of organization. There again, you might not wish to work for a company with such a strange prejudice. However, if you took your earring out for the interview, you could always go back to wearing it when you get the job!

Badges on lapels, men wearing a fistful of rings or medallions and chains around their necks, and women with rings on every finger and chains around their ankles will all be interpreted in some way by an interviewer – and probably none of the interpretations will be favourable or bear any relationship whatsoever to your ability to do the job.

For women, the best advice is to be aware of the culture you are applying to join. In general terms however, you would be advised to keep any jewellery or accessories simple and complimentary rather than excessive, overpowering, noisy and potentially lethal when shaking hands!

Cosmetics

- For cosmetics and make-up, including perfume and body lotions, the advice must be to keep it tasteful and not excessive. For men, it ought to be strictly related to the expectations of the type of organization with whom you are trying to obtain employment. Many interviewers will conjure up negative stereotypes of men who wear make-up. And women would probably be well advised not to over-apply their lipstick, powder, eye shadow and mascara. Some small scale research suggested that women wearing perfume got higher interviewer ratings whilst for men the opposite was true. Not a very world-shattering conclusion and subject, surely, to the type of job and organization for which the people were being interviewed. There is also the possibility that women interviewing women may be influenced by the cost of the perfume being worn – especially if the interviewers couldn't afford it themselves.

The message of this section is, as one sales manager said to me many years ago:

'You only get one opportunity to make a good first impression!'

If you have taken care with your dress and appearance and feel good both inside and outside, this will be noticed by the interviewers and help to put them into a more receptive frame of mind. Dress for what you wish to be and not what you are.

One final tip: Don't forget to arrive in a clean car – especially if you are going to be responsible for a company car. It's all part of your 'first impression'.

Your interaction with other people

How do you think you 'come across' to other people? Have you ever had any accurate and honest 'input on your output'? If you're lucky you get it from your family and close friends. (You'll certainly get it the day you sack someone at work!) Would you be surprised to hear how you would be honestly described by someone who had just met you for the first time? Do you think it would be the way you would describe yourself – or the way you would wish to be seen by others? What self-image do you project? And how might this be affecting your relationships?

Mary was sitting having lunch in the company's restaurant when she was joined by a younger girl – a newcomer to the organization – who asked if she could share the table. 'Please do', said Mary. Their conversation began safely and predictably enough with the weather, the journey to work, the pleasant restaurant and what good value the food was. Mary asked the other girl how long she had been working here because she hadn't noticed her around. 'I only started with the company last week' replied the girl. 'So', said Mary, 'Where had you worked before?' 'I was up the road at the Research Establishment.' 'Oh', said Mary, 'That's where my husband works. Which department were you in?' 'I worked in Personnel', said the girl, 'And where does your husband work?' 'There's a coincidence,' said Mary, 'He works there also!' 'What does he look like?' asked the girl. Mary described her husband. 'Oh', said the girl, 'I know him, he's a bit of a cold fish, isn't he!'

How might you feel if you were thought to be a 'cold fish'? What affect might it have on your relationships if it was true? Have you thought that the 'you' your friends know (and love?) may well be different from the 'you' that other people see for the first time? When did you last have any honest and objective feedback on the impression you make when you meet someone for the first time? It is this first impression that you make on some people which is going to have a very strong influence on your life and your career – especially if those people are the ones who are interviewing you for a job. Or do you think it might be too disturbing to find out? If you don't know, you won't be able to do anything about it. And it may only take a few adjustments in your ways of relating to people to make a great difference to your life and career. Think about it.

What happens in life is that we all develop our favourite communication channels for relating to the world around us in general and to other people in particular.

The following questionnaire will help you to get an idea of what your favourite communication channel(s) might be. There are one hundred short statements with which you may or may not agree. Read each one carefully – but do not spend too much time pondering over them! If you **more or less agree** with any statement or it really does apply to you then **place a tick** beside the statement. If you feel that the statement is not true of you or you **disagree** with it, **do not tick it**. Go through all of the statements as quickly and honestly as you can. Remember, there are no right or wrong answers – only what is true for you. At the end of the questionnaire there are instructions for scoring, preparing your profile and interpreting the results.

■ *The 'Wavelengths' Questionnaire*

ITEM No.	*STATEMENT*	*TICK*
1	*Teenagers would be better advised to try to understand and use the experience of older people.*	☐
2	*Speed limits, rules of the road, the highway code and traffic laws should all be strongly enforced.*	☐
3	*I can appear cool, calm and collected on the outside, even though I may be feeling angry and emotional inside.*	☐
4	*I quite enjoy acting the fool from time to time.*	☐
5	*When I get into awkward, conflict situations with others, I usually seem to come off second best.*	☐
6	*Sometimes I do things and make decisions based on gut reactions and hunches – and it seems to work more often than not.*	☐
7	*I usually think about things and make plans before I act.*	☐
8	*I genuinely respect other people's ideas.*	☐
9	*There are tried and tested ways of doing things and I like to see them being given a chance of working for as long as possible.*	☐
10	*I can usually take a step back from my feelings when I need to.*	☐
11	*If someone keeps trying to tell me what to do all the time, I can get annoyed.*	☐
12	*On the whole it's just as easy to do what you're told.*	☐
13	*I can usually get people to do things for me most of the time.*	☐

14 *I usually take a cool, calm, logical and rational approach to problem-solving.* ☐

15 *The cinema and television seem to show too much harmful sex and violence nowadays.* ☐

16 *I usually push myself harder than I believe most other people push themselves.* ☐

17 *I believe most people are capable of self-determination and self-control.* ☐

18 *It seems to me that other people take life much more seriously than I do.* ☐

19 *It has an effect on me when people show their approval or their disapproval of what I do.* ☐

20 *I like creating or making things with my hands.* ☐

21 *I like reading a lot, especially non-fiction.* ☐

22 *The most important thing is for parents to love their children.* ☐

23 *No one was ever hurt by a few sacrifices.* ☐

24 *I don't seem to have much trouble clearly expressing myself or my ideas.* ☐

25 *I have a tendency to challenge other people in a rather aggressive or questioning manner.* ☐

26 *Humility is one of the greatest virtues.* ☐

27 *Life would be somewhat dull if we always had to do the same things the same way all of the time.* ☐

28 *I rather enjoy going on courses and the like.* ☐

29 *No one is justified in committing suicide even when they feel life is no longer worth living.* ☐

30 *A spell of National Service would do many teenagers a lot of good.* ☐

31 *Being able to keep my cool is much more characteristic of me than becoming angry or frightened.* ☐

32 *I get a kick from driving fast or being in a vehicle which is being driven fast.* ☐

33 *I don't make the rules, I just follow them.* ☐

34 *Sometimes I seem to solve problems by sudden flashes of inspiration which help me to see things in a new light.* ☐

35 *I usually do a lot of fact-finding and making comparisons before I make important purchases like a computer, television, video, stereo or car.* ☐

36 *Some ceremonies, like baptism for instance, are much more than rituals. They play an important part in a person's spiritual welfare.* ☐

37 *They should never completely do away with capital punishment.* ☐

38 *When faced with an opposing point of view I can usually keep an open mind.* ☐

39 *There's nothing better than a good, old-fashioned argument.* ☐

40 *I find that a bit of humour or a joke is useful when situations get a bit heavy or tense.* ☐

41 *Quite often I see different ways of doing things which other people can't.* ☐

42 *I must admit to talking shop and looking at books and magazines when I am at parties.* ☐

43 *I believe that, in life generally, it would be more beneficial for people to seek more than just personal satisfactions.* ☐

44 *Mixed marriages seem to be just asking for problems as far as I'm concerned.* ☐

45 *When other people seem to have lost their concentration, I seem able to maintain mine.* ☐

46 *You can't beat a drink, a good meal and a laugh with friends.* ☐

47 *I don't like seeing people arguing, even when I am not personally involved.* ☐

48 *I find myself wrapped up in my own thoughts and day-dream from time to time.* ☐

49 *Silences and pauses or lapses in conversations don't worry me.* ☐

50 *People often seem to come to me for guidance and direction.* ☐

51 *'Don't rest on your laurels' could be a good motto for most people in business.* ☐

52 *Doing puzzles, quizzes, crosswords and the like are some of my interests.* ☐

53 *People who expect me to be submissive or accept compromise make me angry.* ☐

54 *New and unexpected situations or events make me nervous and uncomfortable.* ☐

55 *I wouldn't mind working at a more creative job if I had a chance.* ☐

56 *When others become somewhat emotional, I seem to be able to stay cool, calm, collected and rational.* ☐

57 *Real leadership is about getting people to give of themselves rather than always seeking to get the best for themselves.* ☐

58 *A good leader is worth ten committees.* ☐

59 *I seem to be able to get along with all sorts of people.* ☐

60 *I like to indulge myself from time to time and can't seem to resist the feeling to do so.* ☐

61 *I seem to have some difficulty in making up my mind at times. I procrastinate and put things off until the last minute.* ☐

62 *I spend a fair amount of time outside work just thinking about ways of doing my job better.* ☐

63 *I do believe that it is possible to be open and honest with other people.* ☐

64 *I believe that bossy people are really lacking in self-confidence – although they may not really realize this.* ☐

65 *I think people should go to church more often.* ☐

66 *When I was younger my parents and teachers encouraged me to explore things, ask questions and try to learn things for myself.* ☐

67 *If someone comes on strong with me, they won't get the best results.* ☐

68 *When I was a child I can remember older people making me feel ashamed of myself and what I had done.* ☐

69 *I read more science fiction and general fiction than non-fiction.* ☐

70 *I seldom blush, if at all.* ☐

71 *I believe there's not much wrong with someone who goes around helping people.* ☐

72 *I like to be in charge and run things.* ☐

73 *Mistakes generally arise from misunderstandings rather than carelessness.* ☐

74 *To live my life on the basis of 'all work and no play' would be pretty dull.* ☐

75 *I sometimes have to tell myself to shut up when I think I am talking too much.* ☐

76 *I believe I genuinely respect other people's opinions.* ☐

77 *I consider that strictly enforced speed limits would help avoid accidents and reduce road deaths.* ☐

78 *I just have to say something when I think someone is wrong or being stupid.* ☐

79 *When I need to, I can always step back and look at things from a rational viewpoint.* ☐

80 *Showing your feelings – affection or anger – as I sometimes do, is OK.* ☐

81 *At some time in my past I have learned to take healthy attitudes towards sex, intimacy and my body.* ☐

82 *I think parents nowadays are too permissive.* ☐

83 *If you want to be successful you must have one thing – discipline.* ☐

84 *I seldom feel bored, impatient or lonely, even when I am with strangers.* ☐

85 *I believe I attend more courses, seminars and the like than most other people I know.* ☐

86 *I feel that more censorship, rather than less, of television, films and magazines, etc, would be good for us.* ☐

87 *You soon find that liberal societies become too free.* ☐

88 *I will speak up for those things in which I believe strongly, but I am also prepared to change my point of view in the face of sound ideas.* ☐

89 *I don't believe that there is a natural or inevitable conflict between the needs of the individual and the organization.* ☐

90 *I value and think that the good opinions of other people are important.* ☐

91 *I like to have rules, precedents and guidelines to follow.* ☐

92 *There are times when I allow myself to feel extremely excited.* ☐

93 *I have at some time had to make myself unpopular to get an important job done.* ☐

94 *If the conditions for getting married were stricter, I believe it would be taken more seriously and the number of divorces would decrease.* ☐

95 *The best way to run a business is to give and get clear instructions.* ☐

96 *Whilst experience is useful, it probably needs to be modified to take account of new ideas and information.* ☐

97 *I like to work out the consequences of my decisions before I take them.* ☐

98 *I believe there are times when you can justify giving a child a good spanking.* ☐

99 *People don't seem to accept responsibility now as much as they once did.* ☐

100 *Even when there are other people around me I am not ashamed to cry if I am happy or sad.* ☐

(This questionnaire has been reproduced with permission from the *Manual for Self-Assessment* published by the Centre for Self Development.)

You are now ready to score, profile and interpret your responses.

■ *Scoring your questionnaire*

For every tick you made on the questionnaire, circle the corresponding number on the list on the facing page.

Add your circles and put the totals in the appropriate sub-total and total boxes.

1
8
15
22
29
36
43
50
57
64
71
77
82
86
90
94
98

Sub-total NURTURING PARENT

2
9
16
23
30
37
44
51
58
65
72
78
83
87
91
95
99

Sub-total CRITICAL PARENT

3
7
10
14
17
21
24
28
31
35
38
42
45
49
52
56
59
63
66
70
73
76
79
81
84
85
88
89
92
93
96
97
100

4
18
32
46
60
74

Sub-total FREE CHILD

11
25
39
53
67
80

Sub-total AGGRESSIVE CHILD

Sub-total F+A=
Sub-total NATURAL CHILD

5
12
19
26
33
40
47
54
61
68
75

Sub-total ADAPTED CHILD

6
13
20
27
34
41
48
55
62
69

Sub-total LITTLE PROFESSOR

TOTAL PARENT

TOTAL ADULT

TOTAL CHILD

Profiling your scores

Parent and Child Sub-totals

Transfer each of the five sub-totals from your scoring guide to the respective columns below:

	PARENT		
	CP	NP	
17			17
16			16
15			15
14			14
13			13
12			12
11			11
10			10
9			9
8			8
7			7
6			6
5			5
4			4
3			3
2			2
1			1
	CP	NP	

	CHILD			
	NC			
12		AC		12
11			LP	11
10				10
9				9
8				8
7				7
6				6
5				5
4				4
3				3
2				2
1				1
	NC	AC	LP	

Parent, adult and child totals

Transfer your separate parent, adult and child total scores to the following boxes. Multiply them by 3 to arrive at the Grand Total, which should then be transferred to the equivalent circle on the following 'targets'. Then trace around the circle on each 'target' and fill in each circle with a felt pen or crayon.

PARENT	ADULT	CHILD
× 3=	× 3=	× 3=

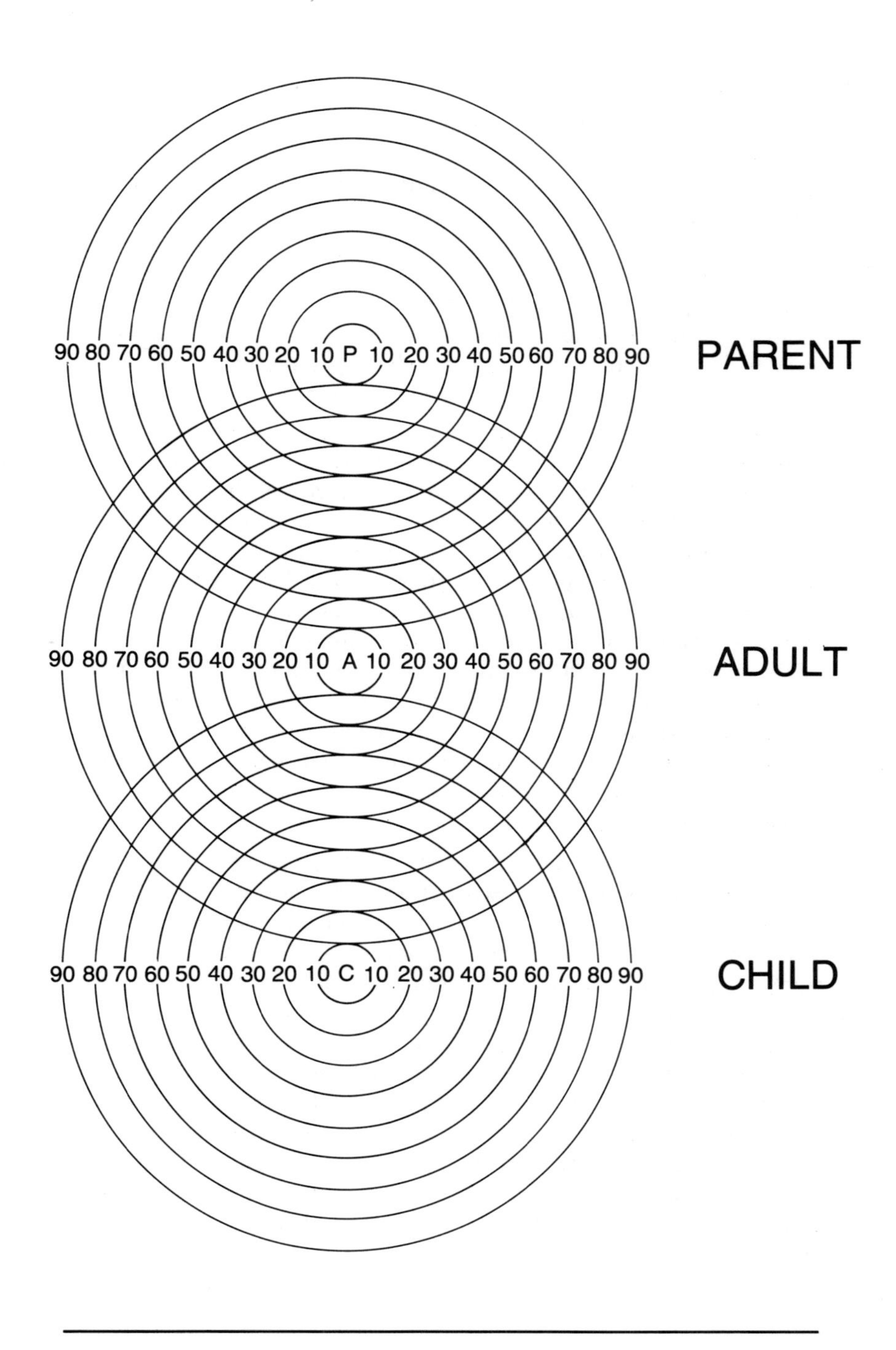
90 80 70 60 50 40 30 20 10 P 10 20 30 40 50 60 70 80 90
PARENT
90 80 70 60 50 40 30 20 10 A 10 20 30 40 50 60 70 80 90
ADULT
90 80 70 60 50 40 30 20 10 C 10 20 30 40 50 60 70 80 90
CHILD

■ ***Interpreting your scores***

This questionnaire is based on the theory of Transactional Analysis. The scores indicate your Ego States, which are ways of referring to your personality traits and your preferred ways of communicating with or behaving towards other people. The idea is that within you are three separate and distinct sources of energy and behaviour called **parent**, **adult** and **child**. These have arisen out of your unique experiences since birth. They developed more rapidly in a more enduring way in your early, formative years than in later life. They represent ways in which you prefer to react to your environment in general and people in particular.

The **parent** represents that part of you containing messages in your memory resulting from your relationships with your parents (or parent figures) when you were small. You recorded in your brain cells your feelings and the thoughts which accompanied your observations and interactions. Many of the things which happened to you then were unexplained by your parents. You were told to do things and it is these unedited experiences which are your memories. Now, although you are grown up, many of your ways of thinking, feeling and reacting are still being influenced by those childhood memories. You act them out in your present life, sometimes regardless of the fact that they are no longer appropriate and even irrelevant to your current needs. The Parent Ego State is your taught way of living which relies on archaic messages stored in your brain cells.

There are two aspects to your parent. Firstly, you have your **critical parent**, consisting of experiences where you were continually told what to do, believe, say and think. Your parents controlled you using whatever means they thought fit – by threats, punishments, constraints. They judged and accused you and used words like 'should' and 'must'. They wagged their fingers, narrowed their eyes, raised their voices and drew themselves up to their full height. They treated you and everyone else like children – irrespective of your ages. And you may now be repeating these behaviours yourself. Your other parent – the **nurturing parent** – is the face of tender loving care which protected you and did things to care for you and comfort you in times of need, when you were frightened, hurt, ill and confused. They provided a warm supportive environment and left you with the capability of doing the same for others if you so choose. So your parent can be judgmental, critical of self and others, moralistic, directive and orientated towards how to do things, rigid, prejudiced, wanting to control others – particularly by invoking feelings of guilt – authoritarian, traditional, possibly loving, warm, caring, supportive and paternalistic.

Your **child** represents the part of you which contains your feelings arising from contacts with your parents and other important figures in your early life. It is the way in which you reacted to what your parents said and did to you when you were small.

Your child has three parts. The first is your free or **natural child**. You were born with a reservoir of energy which expressed itself in joyous, happy ways or in the angry, aggressive, demanding, selfish and intolerant manner of small children. Your elders took you in hand to socialize you so that you could live acceptably in their world. In doing so, they 'knocked you into shape' and developed your **adapted child**. You adapted to survive, get along with and be loved by your parents. This is the part of you which can make you either rebel or conform, stomp off in a temper or sulk when chastised, slam doors behind you or run errands to curry favour. You say 'Sorry', 'won't' or 'shan't', pout your lips, become intransigent and avoid people and problems. The third part of your child is the **little professor**. This is the ingenious part of you with its reservoir of ideas, day-dreams and fantasies which thinks creatively and helps you to manipulate people, just as you were able to do when very young. It's the 'old head on young shoulders' part of you which knows how to get its way with others. Your **child**, therefore, ranges from being spontaneous, fun-loving, creative, fantastic, impulsive, stubborn, rebellious, manipulative, sulking, 'poor me' to being dependent, reactionary, non-conformist, self-centred and self-pitying.

The third ego state is that of your **adult** – the logical, rational, factual, data-processing part of you: your thinking self. This ego state mediates between the intolerant, instant, thoughtless demands or strong desires for a bit of a giggle of your child state and the strict, repressive, play-it-by-the-rules approach and constraints which come from your parent. Your adult is logical, rational, non-emotional, objective, fact-orientated, calculating, funless, ageless, computer-like, probabilistic, constantly up-dating the data, concerned with and orientated towards the reality of 'here and now'. It examines past memories in the light of what is happening now and what needs to happen in the future. It can influence your present behaviour and over-ride inappropriate archaic messages from your parent. The adult is attentive, listening, asking questions, seeking opinions and ideas without making value judgements. It is the problem-solving, decision-making part of you.

You may switch rapidly between Ego States – even within one conversation. The important question is whether you are communicating from the most appropriate 'wavelength' in relation to the situation, the people with whom you are interacting and the purpose of the relationship.

The highest of your three scores is probably the ego state from which you tend to deal with people and the events in your life. You have preferred it, practised it and perfected it from your earliest days. You feel it has stood you in good stead and you would have some difficulty in giving it up. For many people, one of their ego state scores is higher than the others. Where there is a score difference of, say, more than nine points between your highest score and the next lowest score(s), you will probably tend not to use the lower ego state(s) as much as the higher one(s). Where the difference between scores is less than about nine points, it is probable that you can switch between those ego states more readily when you think it is appropriate. In general terms, like most personality characteristics and traits, no single ego state is better than any other, provided you are using it in the right way and at the right time and no one ego state is likely to stand you in good stead in all situations throughout your life.

Your profile and your interview behaviours

By now you will have started to see how your preferred ego states might influence what happens between you and other people during an interview. You may have a sneaking suspicion that you may not be communicating from the most appropriate 'wavelength' and projecting the most attractive aspects of your personality when it is most important that you do so. If 'Man is his own worst enemy', you must ensure that this is not true of you – especially during your job interviews.

It would be nice to be able to say to you that if you stay in 'such-and-such' an ego state, then you will get through your interview successfully. The truth is that, during an interview, whether you are with one person or being confronted by a panel, you may well have to switch from one ego state to another in a short space of time. All ego states have their uses. The difficulty you often have is that if you prefer to operate strongly out of one, you will sometimes find difficulty in switching to others – even if you recognise that a switch is needed. Here are some ideas on what might happen when you come out of one or other of the three main ego states.

- ***Your parent in an interview***

The great danger here – especially if you have a strong critical or controlling parent inside you – is that you might start to take over the interview, wag your finger at the interviewers, glower, admonish them and treat them in a derogatory manner.

'Harold', I asked, 'why do you think you have difficulty in getting second interviews? You seem to do very well in getting through the application and shortlisting stages and get invited to first interviews. What do you think is going wrong?' 'I don't know,' replied Harold, 'I think it's something to do with those stupid personnel types I have to see at the first interview. I mean, they're not the ones who make the important selection decisions, are they? It's the line manager who's really important and the one I want to get in front of, isn't it!'

All of Harold's contempt for 'those stupid personnel types' came through so clearly in his words and body language during this counselling session. Is it difficult to see why he never got beyond the first interview – especially since so many interviews are with the personnel specialists who decide whether or not to pass you on to the ultimate employer – the line manager?

If the interviewers are in a parent state, then they may well expect you to be in compliant child state – a difficult position for a dominant parent candidate to assume. And why should you? If the company wants 'Yes' men and women and you fit that bill – all well and good. But if you are not, then there is unlikely to be a meeting of minds. But, of course, the interviewer's critical parent may bring out your rebellious child – and that's hardly likely to create a smooth dialogue either. Your best bet in this situation is to try to get into and remain in an adult state until the interview is over. You might not get the job, but then perhaps you would feel uncomfortable working in that type of culture. However, you may well be able to find your critical parent fitting in nicely with another autocrat whose views you share!

If your parent state is more nurturing, then you should probably be seeking a culture which has a more ethical basis, a greater concern for people as ends in themselves and not as means to ends, to be manipulated for the good of others. Otherwise, in a 'macho' organizational culture you may well be seen by the interviewers as being too soft for them.

■ ***Your child in an interview***

If your child state is strongly adapted, then you may well come across as a very compliant person with no opinions of your own, prepared to be swayed in whatever direction the interviewers care to take you, unwilling or unable to put and defend a logical point of view different from that of your 'parents' or superiors – the interviewers.

Adopting a rebellious child posture is less likely to endear you to someone during an interview – unless you can bring some adult behaviour into play to moderate the less attractive aspects of the rebel state, which tends not to suffer fools gladly!

For work involved in sales and meeting the public, it may well be to your advantage to have a large, bubbling, fun-loving, hail-fellow-well-met free child to draw upon, as long as you recognize when to be serious and when to inject some humour into the situation. Getting the balance right is important, and 'reading' the situation and the interviewers is critical. The best guide is, when in doubt, take the lead from the interviewers and don't make them the subject of your sense of humour.

A little professor comes into his/her own in those appointments where creativity is sought and encouraged. This is not only in artistic roles, but also in research, development, systems analysis, consultancy and many others where 'breaking with tradition' is essential for success.

■ ***Your adult in an interview***

If your strongest and most preferred ego state is adult, there is a great danger in being seen as a machine rather than as a person – someone without feelings, lacking in humour, unable to understand one's fellow man. However, a positive aspect of being high in the adult state is the potential to cope with more emotional situations by keeping the conversation at a logical level, or getting more emotional people to move away from feelings and look at facts. For most interviews and a wide range of jobs, working from adult can be your best bet. But don't forget to smile now and again and show that there is some warmth, feeling and humour beneath the cold, calculating exterior.

Your profile and your future

In the light of what you have read and been thinking about, you should now review your profile. Can you produce evidence from your life and career which lends support to the brief interpretation given of your particular profile? (Or do you feel that you cannot relate to that profile at all?) Are you able to think of instances when you behaved in some of the ways associated with your strongest ego state(s)? What are the implications for your success during interviews? Will you need to think about developing some aspects of your ego states' profile or learn to control others which may be less than useful, especially during interviews?

It is most important to understand that you choose your behaviour and the way in which you react towards others. In theory, therefore, you need not be stuck with inappropriate behaviours. You can respond from ego state(s) other than your most preferred. The problem is that you will have been practising your preferred behaviour for so long that the habit is hard to break without conscious and deliberate efforts – and also knowing what the appropriate alternatives are. Here is another exercise related to the idea of ego states.

Ego states analysis exercise

In the following space, write a thumbnail sketch of yourself based on your Ego States profile. In particular put down your thoughts on your likely interview behaviours. (You can extend this to work and non-work situations if you wish to!)

Further reading

If you are interested in gaining a better understanding of transactional analysis, this book offers a good introduction to the subject:
I'm OK, You're OK by T.A. Harris, Pan, London 1990

Communicating with words

If it is true that 'Meaning is in the mind of the receiver and not in the message', then it is much more important how your words are perceived than what you actually say. The ways in which you use words may not necessarily be those in which they are understood by the person with whom you are communicating. You have to be careful about the words you use during an interview and how you interpret the words addressed to you. This can be difficult if you feel the pressure is on you both to answer quickly and to keep the conversation flowing.

Ideally you should avoid your own special words or jargon unless they are shared by the interviewers. You should also not drop into dialect unless the interviewers also understand it. An accent may be unimportant for some work and taboo in other appointments. Where the job requires you to meet the public, then it is important that your speech is clear and can be understood readily by the majority of the people with whom you have to communicate. 'RP' (received pronunciation) or 'BBC English' might still be expected of you in some jobs. The way you speak may make a lasting impression upon interviewers which may be to your disadvantage if you do not pay attention to what you say and the way you say it.

If you are applying for a job overseas or if the interview is not conducted in your native tongue, this could cause you difficulties in communicating in what is not your 'first language'. You may often place stress and emphasis on different syllables or parts of a sentence, and in doing so, you may be seen as being more passive or possibly more aggressive than a native speaker. If this is true of you then, it may be useful for you to attend some form of spoken language classes to help improve your self-presentation. It all depends on the type of work for which you are applying. If you cannot communicate with the interviewers, they will have no alternative other than to reject you because there is no mutual bridge over which you can walk towards and communicate with each other.

Verbal communication checklist

In general terms, the advice is:

- Speak clearly.
- Slow down if necessary.
- Avoid talking in a 'thick' accent.
- Don't use unfamiliar words and phrases, i.e. jargon.
- Ensure your pronunciation is correct - especially of foreign words.
- Do not use dialect expressions except when illustrating some relevant point, perhaps in an anecdote.

One way to hear how you might come across to others is to listen to yourself on a tape recorder. Of course that doesn't sound like you to you! That's because you hear yourself internally and not through your ears. Don't cringe because you feel you have an accent. Make sure it works for you and not against you. Perhaps you have to moderate it a little? The important thing to use as your criterion is will the interviewers understand your 'normal self'? If not, what must you do about it? Remember: winners know how to use words.

Your body langauge

Interest in non-verbal or visual behaviours – the body language of human beings – has grown considerably in the past 25 years. This probably stemmed from the work of Albert Mehrabian in the USA, whose research suggested that the greater part of interpretation – probably more than 90% during a face-to-face exchange between people – is due to what I call the 'music' rather than the words, i.e. the accompanying body language. The sort of factors involved in understanding non-verbal communication include the ways in which you walk, touch, make eye contact as well as your gestures, posture and facial expressions.

Interviewers will start to make judgements about you as soon as you enter the room on the basis of what shape you are – and what shape you are in. They will react to you differently, according to the ways in which they interpret your initial impact, often based on generalisation and stereotypes and not founded on any real evidence. They will be forming their first impressions of you – for better or worse. These first impressions are very powerful in influencing their final decisions, however irrelevant they are to successful job performance.

Frederick had been unemployed for many months and had at last obtained an interview. After the initial 'ice breakers' and niceties, the interviewer eventually got around to asking 'How do you feel about not having worked for nearly 18 months?' Frederick's eyes became downcast, his shoulders hunched, hands between his thighs. He slowly assumed a foetal-like posture. He found difficulty in replying. His voice was quiet and low. Some words were difficult to get out. He hesitated frequently. He didn't really need to speak – his body language had said everything for him.

Your body size may be communicating something about you. One theory suggests there are three types of body build: ectomorphs, mesomorphs and endomorphs. If you are an ectomorph then your build will be 'lean and hungry' and you could be seen as a quiet, intellectual and tense sort of person. Mesomorphs are of an athletic or muscular build and may be considered aggressive, adventurous and self-reliant. If you are an endomorph, you will be a somewhat 'Falstaffian figure', inclined towards corpulence and possibly considered warm-hearted, agreeable and a dependent sort of person. There is also some research which suggests a positive correlation between the height of men and the likelihood of being chosen for leadership roles!

Your face will betray your emotions and their intensity will be emphasized by what you do with your arms and the rest of your body. Your emotions will 'leak'. You will be able to lie with your words but your non-verbal language will tell the interviewer what you are really thinking. You will need to ensure that there is congruence between the words and the music: what you say and the way you say it must be in balance. If you are pleased about something, it's no use just saying the words. Make sure your face and body are supporting them. Mixed signals tend to create and maintain negative feelings on the part of the receiver. Avoid them.

Non-verbal behaviour works both ways. You have to be attentive to what the interviewers are doing so you can estimate the impact of your words on them.

Annette was being interviewed for work as a PA to a senior executive. The interviewer asked her to describe her present responsibilities. She did so and mentioned that her present employer was a person of regular habits who liked to start and finish on time, which, Annette said, suited her well because of the circuitous way she had to get to and from work in the rush hour. She preferred not to have to work outside of normal hours. As she said this, she saw the interviewer's eyebrows nearly shoot off the top of his forehead. She immediately added a qualifying comment to the effect that she really had no objection to working later provided she knew about it in advance. Annette had been sufficiently alert to notice that the interviewer's involuntary facial expression had betrayed his surprise or dislike of the information Annette had communicated. His expression had betrayed his unspoken value judgement as loud as any words. She saw this and immediately modified her story, but too late. This particular point was taken up in some depth and it probably led to her not being offered the appointment.

Eye contact is important. Research suggests that if you make contact more than about 65% of the time, you could be making the other person feel uncomfortable. Alternatively, if you make eye contact for less than about 50% of the time, you could be seen as untrustworthy. This might present difficulties if you have been raised, say, in a Middle Eastern culture where it is certainly considered improper to make eye contact with certain people. Downcast eyes are a sign of respect towards someone of higher status. And for women from some cultures this means downcast eyes towards everyone. Increased eye contact in western culture tends to be associated with dominance. If you are Italian you would stare at someone more than a native of the UK might. We might see the Italians as being 'rude' or 'aggressive' and they might see us as 'cold' and 'shifty'!

What you do with your hands and arms may also be given a wide range of interpretations by interviewers. You sit with your arms across your chest, even tucking your hands under your armpits or clenching your fists from time to time. How might this be interpreted? Could you be seen as defensive, 'closed', uncooperative, unreceptive and wanting to withdraw from the conversation? That might be how you feel and your thoughts are betrayed by your body. Conversely, if your arms are slightly outstretched, hands open, palms facing upwards you are probably communicating a desire to be open and cooperative with nothing to hide.

People from different cultures have different ideas on personal space and these have been 'plotted' in various research projects. If the interviewers move closer towards you, this could suggest that the level of trust is increasing, but it might make you feel uncomfortable if they get too close. If you are from, say, Mediterranean countries and the Middle East you will feel more comfortable being closer to someone than if you are native British. If you have travelled widely on holiday or business you will be well aware of national and cultural differences in this idea of personal space.

Crossing your arms and legs accompanied by a stony facial expression is a give-away indication of being unreceptive, suspicious, feeling insecure and having a need to protect yourself. Somewhere between being in a catatonic state and emulating a human windmill, there is a happy medium for what to do with your body. Interest and enthusiasm are often indicated by moving towards the interviewer, possibly even to the edge of the seat, smiling, eyes lighting up, more animated speech. And, of course, the exact opposite will probably demonstrate your complete disinterest in the job.

If you look intently at the interviewer, tilt your head slightly on one side and stroke your chin, then the message is that you're interested and thinking about what was said. But if you rock or sit back a little on your chair, place your hands behind your head and look down your nose at them . . . Well, I think that clearly communicates how you feel about the interviewers and the situation! And look out for the interviewer's jaw drop which tells you that what you have said has just surprised them. If the interviewers take off their spectacles, slowly fold and unfold their legs, try to conceal a yawn, or look out of the window, perhaps you'd better think about bringing things to a close, or try more succinct or interesting responses.

Try placing your hand over your heart when you want to communicate your sincerity, honesty or loyalty. It helps to support the words. And if the interviewers can't look directly at you when talking about your prospects, or what happened to the last incumbent, you should doubt what they are saying, but don't fall into the same traps yourself! Maintain a conversational style, speaking with the volume turned down and a low pitch with few alterations to these patterns throughout. This can be interpreted as meaning that you are better educated, more in control, trustworthy, confident and more professional.

Avoid fidgeting in your chair because the interviewer(s) may mistake this for nerves or that you feel uncomfortable and under pressure. Of course there could be other reasons of which they are not aware. Try not to pull yourself up to your full height and tower over the interviewers – whether they are standing or seated – since this is a sign that you wish to dominate them and consider yourself to be superior. Perhaps you do, but is it wise to communicate this so loudly?

Don't get anything into your hands when you are being interviewed, like a pen or pencil or paper clip. If you start to play with these it could indicate your anxiety or lack of security – nervous energy looking for an outlet. It may also distract the interviewers. Drumming fingers, waggling toes, clicking ballpoint pens in and out, doodling and tapping feet could all be give away signs of impatience or boredom. If they do that, then try to speed up the conversation or get them more involved – perhaps you are talking too much or talking rubbish.

The thing to be wary of is inferring complex human motives from isolated pieces of body language. There needs to be a 'cluster' of behaviours accompanied with suitable words before you can confidently interpret what people are telling you non-verbally. Unfortunately, many interviewers will be making their judgements on isolated incidents which might have a number of different underlying causes. If you do too many of the following, you may well be labelled as a liar or untrustworthy:

- Give off different signals where the words and the music are out of balance.
- Don't have any body language whatsoever – or very little.
- Perspire, gulp, shake and speak with a tremor in your voice.
- Fiddle with pens and things all of the time.
- Keep shuffling your feet and changing the position of your legs.

- Blush, keep touching your nose or eyes and licking your lips.

You could also be on the outlook for the same sort of signs from your interviewer(s).

Head up, shoulders back, a purposeful step, good eye contact, a pleasant greeting and being well turned out will all help to increase the likelihood of you being accepted more readily, but only if you are equally articulate. Appropriate body language is not a substitute for being inarticulate and answering questions badly.

The skilled interviewer may also be looking out for two other aspects of communication, which are often included in the realm of body language. These are sub-vocals and vocalism. Sub-vocals are saying things like 'Um, aha, mmm' and the like. They usually communicate either that you understand – if accompanied by suitable head-nodding – or that you are thinking about what has been said. You should use these when appropriate to let the interviewer know that they are communicating with you.

Vocalism is when you place emphasis on different words in a sentence. You will recognize this – try saying the following sentence several times emphasizing one word in turn more strongly than the rest on each occasion and see how it affects the conveyed meaning: 'Naturally, I really enjoy my work.' See how important emphasis is when communicating. Make sure you are communicating what you intend.

Body language checklist

Think about these aspects of your first impressions and body language:

- Dress in a way which is in keeping with the culture you are in and the job for which you are being interviewed. If necessary find out what the accepted standards are beforehand.
- Touch is important. Start positively with a good, firm handshake.
- When walking and standing, keep reasonably erect. When seated, don't lean too far forward or backward nor adopt a bolt upright position. Try to open up your body and only move forward when you want to show interest.

- Get as close as you can without giving the interviewers the feeling that you are aggressively invading their personal space.
- Give the interviewer as much eye contact as you can – to catch their attention, when you are speaking to them, when you would like to get into the conversation, but don't stare them out.
- Let your face come alive. Smile in a friendly manner without maintaining a fatuous grin all the time.
- Use your head to indicate that you are listening, understanding, being attentive. Cock your head slightly to one side or the other from time to time. Don't let your chin drop into your neck. It's neither good for projecting your voice nor giving an impression that you are feeling confident and on top of things.
- If you wish to give the impression that you are searching your memory for or trying to construct images and responses to questions, look up to your right or left.
- Try to maintain open postures with your hands, arms and body. Don't fold and cross arms, clench and unclench fists, fidget too much. Use these parts of your body to help express yourself without simulating a windmill in a Force 9 gale or a bookmaker five seconds before the start of the race.
- Try not to talk too fast or too slowly. You will be appreciated best if you can divide your time more or less equally between being seen to listen and talking. Make sure that you can be heard without deafening the interviewer(s) and are modulating your voice a little from time to time for the sake of emphasis and variety.
- Avoid dialect and strong regional accents unless these are understood by the interviewers and would be acceptable in the job for which you have applied.

■ *Further reading*

If you are interested in studying this subject in greater depth try reading *Manwatching* and *Bodywatching* by Desmond Morris, published by Jonathan Cape, London.

Your listening skills

Your listening skills are important. Possibly for as much as half of the interview time you will be required to listen. Ideally a trained interviewer will be encouraging you to talk more than half of the time. It is said of salesmen that, if they can't listen, how on earth can they sell anything to anyone? And you really are a salesman in an interview. Only by listening can you discover what other people want and how you can satisfy their needs. It is not sufficient to be a good listener, you must also demonstrate visually that you are listening. This is where your knowledge of body language is extremely important.

It is vital that you remain an attentive listener throughout your interview. You cannot afford to let your thoughts wander off onto any of your 'hidden agendas' – the other things on your mind which are unrelated to what is going on in front of you. If you are unclear about what has been said to you or asked of you, then check your understanding or ask for the question to be repeated. It is better to ask for clarification than to answer the wrong question.

Listening skills checklist

As a good listener you will:

- Make eye contact.
- Slightly cock your head on one side or the other from time to time and possibly nod up and down to show agreement and understanding.
- Occasionally utter sub-vocal noises like 'aha', 'mmm', 'um', etc.
- Let the speaker talk without interrupting.
- From time to time, ask for clarification of what has been said.
- Keep your prejudices and emotions under control.
- Sometimes re-phrase what has been said to you so you can check with the speaker that you have correctly understood what was said.
- Keep your mind open until the speaker has finished and don't try to evaluate what is being said halfway through the statement.

Listening may not come easily to you. We all tend to be 'selective listeners': we don't hear some things because they are unimportant or threatening or we are concentrating on listening for what we want to hear. If you are dominant or extrovert, you may tend to like more 'air time' than others and thus you may not be so good at listening. If you are very self-confident this may also militate against you wanting to listen to other people and their ideas. Active listening is a much-valued skill in many occupations and demonstrating it could well help you make a favourable impression during your interview.

This chapter has looked at your initial impact and stressed how important it is to get this right for the occasion. It then suggested that you need to look at the way in which you communicate with others in terms both of your ego states and the words you use. The messages conveyed through your non-verbal behaviours have also been considered and, finally, the importance of being a good listener. Attention to all of these points will help to enhance your self-presentation and make a good impression.

4 How should I prepare for the interview?

'Knowledge is of two kinds: we know a subject ourselves, or we know where we can find information upon it.'

Samuel Johnson

You know that interviewers have expectations of and criticisms about the way in which you present yourself. They are interested in finding something out about you as an individual and how well you could do their job. Your preparation, therefore, must concentrate on meeting their expectations, overcoming their criticisms and persuading them that you are their 'ideal' candidate. In this chapter we shall cover briefly what you need to do when you receive your invitation before we look at your preparation, which will include thinking about the job and you, your career, the organization, questions you should ask and your motivation. Finally, we look at different ways in which you can rehearse for your interview.

Invitations

If you have been shortlisted you may receive a telephone call, or more usually a written invitation, to the next part of the assessment process, which may be one of a number of activities, such as:

- Telephone shortlisting interview.
- Face-to-face 'screening' interview.
- Graduate 'milk-round' discussion on campus.

- Visit to the company's stand and meet its representatives at a graduate hiring fair.
- Visit to the organization on an Open Day.
- Testing session which might last for up to a day.
- Visit to one of the company's locations for a tour.
- Final selection interview.
- Comprehensive Multiple Assessment Centre.

Where overnight accommodation is necessary, the organization usually makes the arrangements for you at their expense and you merely sign the account at the hotel when you depart. Details of allowable expenses and methods of claiming are usually included with invitations. Good practice is for organizations to allow you to reclaim reasonable travelling expenses and necessary overnight accommodation. If in doubt, you should always check with them beforehand. It may be helpful if you can re-arrange your interview time to obviate an overnight stay. Don't claim first class fares and travel as economically as possible. It's not unusual for the organizations to check on this and is it worth the risk of losing a job offer for the sake of a few pounds and the way it might reflect on you?

If you have any personal needs or disabilities, forewarn the organization as soon as possible. They may be able to assist in a variety of ways such as with diet, organizing access for wheelchairs and providing dictation facilities or a shorthand writer, etc.

Larger organizations may send comprehensive information packs with their invitations. These often contain a job description, person profile, details of the company, conditions of employment and a map. If you have not received any additional information and feel this could be useful, telephone them see what else there is available. You won't know if you don't ask. If you seek additional information you may be advised that everything has appeared in the advertisement or that you have had whatever there is. It is possible that someone in the Personnel Department may be able to answer some of your questions so have a list ready. You may be passed through to the department with the vacancy and have to speak to the manager or someone else in the department. Don't be reluctant to try and get further information. They might feel a bit put out by your enquiry – especially if they haven't got any more information to give you. But it could also be interpreted as demonstrating initiative and interest on your behalf, which can't be bad. They can't have it both ways.

If you are invited and cannot attend when requested, you may well lose the opportunity. You should always contact them to see if alternative arrangements are possible. If they can accommodate you, it may indicate that you are a strong contender.

Preparing for your interview

As soon as the invitation arrives you should commence your preparation. If you have obtained your interview as a result of making a direct approach to an organization, which may not have advertised any vacancies, you will already have undertaken a great deal of the preparation outlined below.

The job and you

If there is no information pack or any more information other than the advertisement to help you understand the job more thoroughly, there are a number of things you can do. Go and talk to someone who does this type of work, perhaps someone known to you as a friend or member of the family. Call in to your local library or careers office. They have dozens of booklets or pamphlets about different occupations and also a variety of career encyclopedias which describe jobs, including a book called *Standard Occupational Classification* (SOC) published in two volumes by HMSO in 1990 which contains many hundreds of job descriptions. At your local Careers Office ask to use a computer-based program such as *Microdoors with Opendoors*, which has descriptions of hundreds of jobs and is reasonably 'user-friendly'.

Whatever information you require, here are three practical approaches to help you prepare. These have been developed over the past twenty years whilst working with life and career changers and hundreds of unemployed supervisory, managerial, executive and professional people who found them helpful when preparing for job interviews. The three approaches are know thyself, brainstorming and job match analysis.

However, before we look at them, I ought to mention briefly what I call the 'play it by ear' school. This usually means you don't do anything – or the very minimum you think you can get away with.

It is one of the major criticisms interviewers have of you. It is based on the belief that no preparation or thought is necessary and you will be able to cope with and handle anything that is thrown at you when you get to the interview. I don't believe it and neither should you. Lack of preparation may have got you a job when there were only half a million people unemployed. It's certainly not true nowadays when the competition is stronger.

- ***Know thyself***

  This approach results in you being able to talk about any aspect of you and your life easily and openly at the drop of a hat. You can retrieve from your memory any appropriate response to the questions put to you. To do this you must have spent time thoroughly analysing yourself – either by working through self-assessment exercises or having undergone professional vocational guidance or career counselling. By one means or another you must systematically have reviewed your life and be able to talk easily about yourself without hesitation, repetition or deviation.

  I have suggested that interviewers are often trained to use a biographical interview covering your early background, education and qualifications, occupational training and work experiences, life and interests outside school and work, your present circumstances and where you want to go to in the future.

  They will not necessarily follow this approach rigidly, but during the interview they will need to cover all these areas. If this is a common approach, then one important way of preparing yourself is to use it as a framework for your own self-analysis and preparation. A useful tactic is to be able to talk about each of the above by thinking of them as episodes in your life, as suggested in Chapter 2. You will be then be able to reply easily to requests such as:

  'Tell me about your early days/schooling/qualifications/outside interests/present job, etc.'

  Another way of preparing yourself to respond fluently to this type of interviewing tactic is to keep a copy of your application form and use this for your preparation. Better still, prepare a really comprehensive CV. Make it longer than one you would have printed and sent to an organization. Don't miss anything out. Make it into a mini-autobiography. The important point to note about this form of preparation is that you only have to do it once in some depth. After that it is a matter of updating it and using it to revise for subsequent interviews.

- ***Brainstorming***

This is a technique with which you are probably be familiar. It's a question of 'freewheeling' intellectually – 'Mind in top gear and mouth in neutral!' On a sheet of paper and with the advert in front of you, write down everything you think you could be asked during the interview. Don't question anything you are writing – just get it down on paper. Get a member of the family or a friend to join in the brainstorm, provided you remind them of the 'rules' beforehand. You'll probably dry up after a few minutes. When you have your list, start to put some structure on it – some categories or ways of classifying the questions. Then you read through each of them and decide how you might respond.

- ***Job match analysis***

You may have received a copy of a formal job description, or you may only have the brief details given in the advertisement or details provided by an agency. Whatever you have, use it as the basis of your preparation by doing a job match analysis. You need to do this for *every* interview you attend. It is a simple but powerful approach recommended for developing custom-made CVs and application letters. You may already have used it for these stages in your job hunting. It is essential prior to the interview.

- ***Job match analysis exercise***

On a sheet of A4 paper, draw a vertical line down the centre and write THE JOB at the top of the left-hand column and ME at the top of the right, as shown below.

THE JOB	*ME*

Get out your job correspondence folder in which you file the advert, any organizational information and job description or personnel specification you have received or researched. Read through everything and underline anything related to the responsibilities of the job and the qualifications, training, previous experience, personal characteristics, etc, required of the job holder.

List these as bullet points or key words in the left-hand column with a few lines' space between each. Now go through them one at a time and write what you have done or possess against each one in the right-hand column. You finish with a match between you and the job. Keep going back to it and adding/amending what you have written down.

Develop some questions which you are likely to be asked by the interviewers to get you talking about the issues you have listed in the left hand column. For example, if the advertisement or the job description mentions that the job-holder is going to be involved in managing change, then it would be remiss of you not to prepare yourself to answer the following type of questions:

'What changes have you managed?'
'Why were they necessary?
'How do you go about managing change generally and in this instance?'
'What problems were encountered and solved?'
'What was the end result?'
'What did you learn of value for the next time you have to manage change?'

Your career

The interviewers expect you to have thought of the future – ideally a future with them. Have you ever thought about your future in terms of objectives which are 'SMART' – **S**pecific, **M**easurable, **A**chievable, **R**ealistic and **T**ime-Related? Have you tried to move steadily towards making them come true? Or is this something you usually avoid? The relevant and predictable question is:

'What do you expect to be doing in 'x' years time?'

Perhaps you have worked your way through some form of self-assessment workbook and arrived at your own answer, or maybe you have discussed your career with a Careers Officer or Adviser from the local Education Authority or your college or university?

You may have paid for professional vocation or career counselling. (Names and addresses of your local Chartered Occupational Psychologist offering this service can be obtained from The British Psychological Society, St Andrews House, 48 Princess Road East, Leicester, LE1 7DR Tel: 0533 549568.)

Thinking about the future is dreaming. Dreams are the starting point and raw material of future success. Plans are what make dreams come true. Try the following exercise in 'Futurology'. What you discover about yourself will be invaluable if you have to start answering questions about your career plans.

'My ideal job'
PART I

Imagine that in two or three years' time you will be receiving a letter inviting you to apply for your ideal job. Draft out what the letter will say. It should include information on at least the following points:

1 Job title

2 Salary range

3 Location

4 Type of business, industry or technology

5 Five key results or contributions expected of the job-holder

-
-
-
-
-

6 Five most important personal characteristics, qualities, abilities or experiences required of the successful job-holder

-
-
-
-
-

(NB: This may or may not be a job which actually exists at the present time. The only 'feet on the ground' requirement of this job is that it must be suitable for someone of your age, i.e. not a job requiring you to be an 18-year-old school leaver when you are, in fact, much older!)

Do not try to complete part II of this exercise until you have written this letter to yourself!

PART II

Now that you have written and received the letter inviting you to apply for your ideal job, answer the following questions:

1 How ready am I to perform my ideal job?

2 If I am not yet ready, what do I need to do which is within my control to prepare myself for it?

3 If I am ready now, what am I doing to get it?

4 Do I really enjoy those things most required in this job?

5 Which of the things I value in life may be satisfied by doing this job and which may I have to sacrifice or compromise to do it?

6 Is this job simply a dream or is it something I really could attain?

7 What am I prepared to change or do, if anything, to increase my chances of getting a job I really would like to do in the next two or three years?

(This exercise is reprinted with permission from the *Manual for Self Assessment* published by the Centre for Self Development, Leamington Spa.)

The organization

There are several reasons why you should get to know as much as you can about the organization before your interview. Your natural anxieties about stepping into the unknown can be reduced. You will be better able to emphasize those aspects of your personality and track record which you think are more relevant to their job and the type of person they want to employ. It will help you decide the questions you want answering and the areas you wish to explore with the interviewers, which makes you appear to be a thoughtful, interested and highly motivated candidate. You will be able to create a good overall impression, which might just sway the final selection decision in your favour. It may also help you to make the decision of whether or not to continue with your interest in the company and also whether or not to accept any future offer of employment.

So what might it be advisable to know about the organization and where can you find it? The type of information which seems to be appropriate and useful when building up a picture of an organization includes:

Headquarters and location(s)
Names of directors and senior functional executives
Telephone and fax numbers
Type of ownership – public, private, family, etc

Parent, affiliated or subsidiary companies
International connections, if any
Technologies and processes used
Range of products, goods and/or services
Markets and market shares – home and overseas
Competition
Financial standing and recent results
What the financial institutions think about it
Stated 'mission' or business purpose and aims
Its views about future developments
What its employees think about it
Its standing in the community
Stated or inferred opportunities, changes and problems it is facing or might have to face in the near future
Views on its products, trading methods, and services expressed by customers, suppliers, distributors and competitors

(If there are other aspects you would wish to know about, just add them to this list as you think of them.)

You might feel it a daunting, even impossible, task to get answers to them. You may already have researched most of these if you are using the pro-active approach to job hunting. It will probably not be necessary to find out this much detail about a prospective employer who has invited you to an interview for a more junior post – although it might certainly make you more impressive during the interview. However, the higher you are aiming, the more you will need to explore the organization in the detail indicated here. The depth at which you research an organization will also be influenced by the type of appointment you are applying for or function for which you are being interviewed. Don't despair or feel swamped. There are several ways to find out about these matters. And once you have researched one organization, you will know how to do others when necessary.

Getting answers to some of these will be easy and the sources somewhat obvious. They can be gleaned by keeping your eyes and ears open – walking about, listening and talking to people and reading the local, national and specialist press. Other answers can be found in a few easily-accessible publications in your local library. Some larger organizations, local government, civil service departments and further and higher education institutions often include a mass of information. A telephone call to the Company

Secretary of a PLC will usually produce a free copy of their latest annual report. Most careers offices and the careers units in colleges and universities will let you look through their range of company information. Your local library may also have a more limited supply of information about local organizations to which you can refer.

If it is a local organization, walk around its perimeter. If it is a retail outlet, go inside. If it is not, find out if visits are permitted. There is little excuse if you are an interested and motivated person in not finding out a great deal about a local organization you wish to join. Even if you have some distance to travel, you can consider making a private trip – perhaps with your partner and family – to see what the area is like and also to check out their location and your journey time. Some organizations include the opportunity for a preliminary visit as part of the shortlisting procedure. However, this does not mean that it would not be worthwhile doing some research before you go. You could always arrive early for your interview and have a look around the area and the organization.

If the organization produces consumer goods or offers services to the public, you may be able to inspect them or find out about them by talking to people or by getting copies of promotional materials. Friends or family might have some first or second-hand experiences they will share with you. Perhaps you know someone who knows someone who works for the organization? (Be aware that local government do not like you to 'canvas' their employees about advertised appointments. This may even disqualify you.)

■ ***Researching a specific organization***

Where would you find the following information on a company which has just invited you to an interview:

- Address
- Telephone and fax numbers
- Names of Directors and Senior Executives
- Financial information such as share issues and profitability
- Range of products
- Future developments
- Recent changes in policies and finances

See if you can find more than one source for each of the above.

Inevitably there will be some information which is difficult to find. Directories could be your main source of information.

You could start with *Current British Directories*, which is a directory of directories published by CBD Research, Beckenham, Kent. In addition to the above, you will find the following a useful but by no means exhaustive list.

Britain's Privately Owned Companies

Directory of British Associations, which gives details of more than 6,000 specialist Associations

Kelly's Manufacturers and Merchants Directory, which lists more than 80,000 companies who offer industrial services

Major Companies of Europe gives details of more than 4,000 of the largest Western European companies, such as their activities, senior executives and finances

McCarthy UK Quoted and Unquoted Services

The City Directory has invaluable information on finance sector organizations

The Times 1,000 lists the UK's 1,000 largest companies by turnover

Your local reference library will also be able to suggest other similar books.

Another approach to researching a company is shown on p. 93.

Your own questions

You may have had many of your questions answered before you arrive at the interview in the documentation provided by the organization. Some of them may be answered voluntarily during the interview, but it is still wise to have a checklist of the things of interest to you. It will provide you with some prompts when they ask you, 'Are there any questions you have about the job or the company?' You must develop your own unique list, but some of the issues you might wish to consider are:

'What sort of training might I get?'
'Would the company support any further education I might be interested in/postgraduate/post-experience studies?'

An algorithm for researching company information

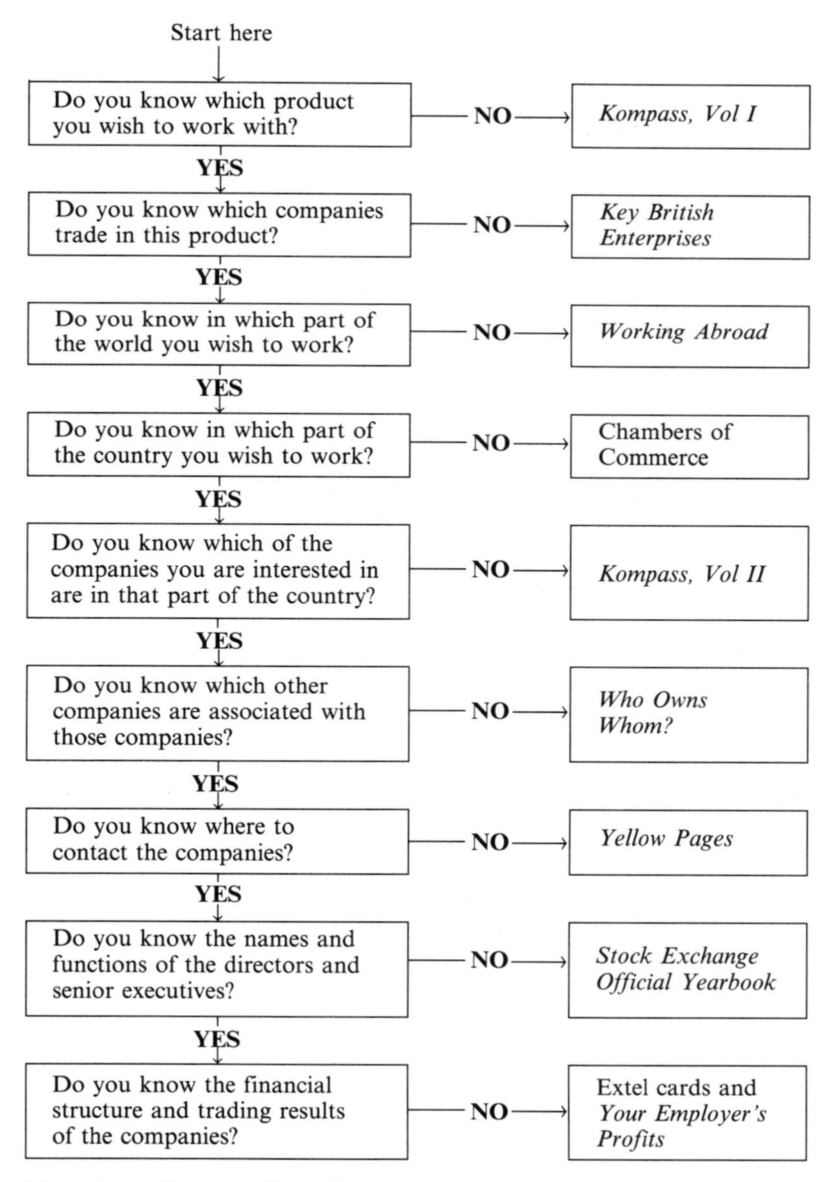

Your local library will probably be able to obtain copies of these or similar books for you.

'Who will I report to?'
'What are the prospects like?'
'In what ways is the organization likely to change over the next few years?'
'When can I expect to hear from you?'
'When would you like me to start?'
'I have already booked some holidays. Can I still take them?'
'What happened to the last incumbent?'

Write these as one-word 'prompts' on a small slip of paper and refer to them when asked during the interview. It indicates that at least you have thought about the organization and the job. But don't make a big thing of it: 'Thank you. You have already provided a lot of information but I was wondering about . . .'

Your interview motivation

In addition to the preparation already recommended, you should try the following exercise. On a separate sheet of paper, answer the following questions:

Interview motivation exercise

1 Motivation
Why am I especially interested in this appointment? (Write down specific reasons and not just generalizations)

2 Relevant experience
What have I got and/or done which fits in with what the organization are seeking or what I believe they require? Make this a more general assessment *before* you get down to doing your detailed preparation and the job match analysis exercise (see p. 84).

3 Related issues
What other 'unique selling points' do I believe I have in relation to this particular appointment which they have not specifically requested?

4 Weaknesses
What do I predict they will question me about which I feel does *not* fit their job description or personnel specification?

(The above exercise is reproduced with permission from *Job Hunter: a definitive guide to job hunting* published by Centre for Self Development, Leamington Spa.)

Rehearsing for your interview

As a result of the activities in this chapter and chapters 1 and 2, you will have numerous ideas of what you are likely to be asked and ways in which you could respond. However, in the last resort, all answers must be tailor-made by you at the time of asking. You must feel comfortable with what you are saying and be able to develop your own replies when probed by the interviewers. You should think about and develop your own strategies for responding to questions rather than try to memorize specific answers. It would not be too difficult for an interviewer to spot it if you were merely regurgitating someone else's ideas. The ideas would come across in a mechanical, unemotional and superficial manner which communicates no real impression of you as a thinking, feeling human being. In any case, you would still have to deal with any follow-up or probing questions or requests for clarification. There is no substitute for having your own responses to whatever questions you may be asked. Use the ideas already provided as thought-provokers rather than 'scripts' to be memorized and repeated 'parrot-fashion'.

There are a number of things you can do to make best use of all this preparation. You can rehearse alone or with the help of others. Independently read through the different questions which have been listed in previous chapters. Select those which you feel specifically apply to a particular interview and think through or write down your answers to them.

With the help of a tape recorder or a video camera and a friend, colleague or member of the family, simulate a 'mock' interview. Select a number of questions you think you might be asked, write them on separate slips of paper, give them to your helper and ask them to pose the questions to you randomly so you won't know what to expect next. Or you could give them the advert, any job or person profile provided by the organization and a copy of your application form and let them develop a number of questions to put to you.

Record these 'interviews' and afterwards review your audio or video tapes and think about ways of improving your answers. Consider repeating the exercise using a mixture of some of the previous questions plus some new ones.

There are two further ways in which you can get help in improving your interviewee skills. The first is to contact local colleges, residential training establishments, universities or similar institutions and volunteer to be a 'guinea pig' on interviewing skills training programmes they run. You must ensure, however, that they give you some feedback on your performance and let you see any tapes they have made. Whilst their concern is to develop the interviewing skills of their trainees, you can improve your own techniques if you can get useful feedback from them. Alternatively you could pay for the services provided by specialist agencies, which can include 'simulated' interviews using video, personal feedback and suggestions on how to improve your technique.

There are different views on which is the 'best' position or time to be allocated in a interviewing schedule. Is it to be the first of the day, or last, or somewhere between? Should you avoid 'death hour' after the interviewer(s) have had a heavy lunch and are semi-comatose? Arguments can be found for both the first and last schools of thought.

A 'Primacy' effect possibly operates for the first candidate. If you are first you set a standard against which everyone else may be measured. The alternative assumes a 'Recency' effect: interviewer(s) will remember you if you are last because there are no further 'inputs' to confuse their memory of you. There is also the possibility of a 'Contrast' effect. This supposes that, if you are sufficiently different from other candidates, you will be more memorable. It could well be true that appearing towards the end of the day's timetable you will have to face some form of 'fatigue factor'. But then you may also be able to bring some light and joy into what has been for the interviewers a pathetic parade of perfectly pallid people!

These alternatives appear to assume that the interviewers either do not have any 'ideal' candidate derived from job analysis and personnel specification or that they do have a person profile but are going to ignore it. In theory, therefore, where you appear should not be relevant to the final decision. In practice, it could well be. However, the above comments also ignore two kinds of research findings. The first is that some research studies suggest information reviewed and images formed before the interview correlate highly with the final decision made, i.e. interviewers make up their minds before they see the candidates and then use specific interviewing tactics to make their pre-judgments come true. The second is that many selection decisions are supposedly made within four and eleven minutes of the start of the interview. Even this is not an invariable practice of all interviewers. What we do not have are sufficient hard facts to confirm what is the 'best' interview position – only lots of individual experiences. My feeling is that, whatever your position in the batting order, you should always try to give of your best.

This chapter has been aimed at helping you to prepare for your interview in such a way that you create the best possible impression of yourself and convince the interviewers that you are their ideal choice. It has been about how you can make yourself attractive to the people who have to make the 'purchasing' decision. The following checklist should be reviewed whenever you receive your invitation and are about to start your preparation.

Pre-interview checklist

These are all basic common-sense tips worth reviewing when your invitation arrives and you have to start your preparation:

- Check the day and date – sometimes they are not compatible. Ensure that there are no calendar or typographical errors.
- Make sure you are free and you have noted the date in your diary.
- See if they need you to acknowledge that you will attend or are working on the assumption everything is OK unless they hear from you to the contrary. If you are not going to attend or anticipate being late then be courteous enough to let them know as soon as possible.
- Check the time (see note on p.97). Is it possible to arrive on time by whatever method of travel you use? Would re-timing the interview save the organization overnight stays before or after the interview? Would changing the time by an hour or so in either direction make it easier if you are using public transport and 'safer' if travelling by road? (By 'safer' I mean more predictable because of the traffic on and state of our roads and motorways.) Sell any changes as benefits for the organization and not just yourself.
- Check passport, currency and tickets for overseas interviews.
- Do you know where to go to? Are the instructions clear and understandable? Have they enclosed a map? What about parking facilities? Is it in a city centre? Should you review and revise your method of travel?
- Draw up your itinerary with mileage, approximate timings and town/city plans where necessary.
- Is an overnight stay necessary and who makes the accommodation arrangements and pays for them?

- What arrangements are there for claiming expenses? If you have to pay for fares, check on your permitted class of travel and if there are expense limits or fixed allowance levels. Check by telephone if necessary.
- Do you have to take anything with you – work specimens, proof of qualifications, references, overnight clothes, waterproofs/heavy shoes for outdoor activities?
- Check that your clothes are (dry) cleaned, pressed and presentable. Think about taking extra clothes just in case of emergencies.
- Start your preparation – get out all correspondence, e.g. advert, job details, information pack.
- If necessary, visit the local library to refer to other sources or retailers, etc who may deal in the products.
- Complete any pre-work required of you, e.g. reading, case studies, presentations, briefs, etc.
- Work out your short 'stories' related to different periods of employment.
- List your predictable questions and work through the answers yourself or with your 'helper'.
- Organize a rehearsal with your 'helper'.
- Work out the questions you want to ask your interviewer(s).

By now you will have thought about, read, written, re-read and generally manipulated your information on numerous occasions. It is now starting to come together in your head and will be more readily recalled when necessary. This leads us to the interview itself.

5 What are interviews like?

'. . . it is a tale, told by an idiot, full of sound and fury, signifying nothing . . .'

Macbeth Act V, Scene V
William Shakespeare

There is no single 'best way' of conducting an interview. The Institute of Personnel Management provides professional guidance in their Code of Practice, but thousands of smaller and medium-sized organizations do not have professional personnel staff. Nor does every interviewer in an organization with a Personnel Department necessarily follow 'good practice'. And there are hundreds of 'occasional' interviewers in geographically-dispersed locations well away from the influence of personnel departments who conduct interviews and may have had little or no training to do so. Many of them believe it is no more than commonsense, requiring no special skills.

After some general observations about the interview, this chapter looks at its shortcomings as a selection method. It then moves on in a more or less chronological sequence to consider the day of the interview before looking at the where, what and how of interviews in some detail. Comments are included on why certain strategies and tactics are being used and ways in which you can try to optimize your participation in them. Screening, stress and telephone interviews are mentioned. Different approaches to structured interviewing are also covered. The chapter closes with comments on the growing use of Multiple Assessment Centres to supplement the traditional selection interview.

My intention is to provide you with as many options as possible about the ways in which you could be interviewed. I do not know in what proportions these alternatives are used. All I do know is that they are being used and that you will undoubtedly be confronted by one or more of them when you are interviewed. I should always be pleased to hear about interesting alternatives!

The selection interview

The selection interview is a two-way communication process with three major purposes of:

- obtaining information from you about your suitability;
- giving information to you about the work and the organization;
- leaving you with a favourable impression of the organization.

The third aim is especially important for the organization since, at some time, you may become a customer, shareholder, supplier or distributor. You are a potential source of good or bad publicity.

The interview is a necessary activity to 'round out' the impersonal and inanimate information obtained from your letters, application forms and references and is invaluable in:

- checking the accuracy of your statements – especially about relevant personal and work-related achievements;
- clarifying and elaborating upon information you have already provided;
- getting you to fill in missing or unexplained 'gaps' in chronology;
- assessing your initial impact and social acceptability in relation to the requirements of the job;
- checking your verbal and interpersonal skills.

It is based on the premise that your behaviour can be predicted from past performance, present circumstances and future expectations and these are best be explored face-to-face.

Interviews are the most favoured method of assessing people for jobs in many countries and it is difficult to see them being replaced. Could you or would you want to join an organization that didn't want to meet you face-to-face beforehand?

A minority of vacancies are probably filled without interviews. This might happen if you were to be given an internal promotion.

For certain appointments or work overseas, the organization may well wish to meet your spouse or partner. Work in residential training establishments, social service establishments or institutions, in the hotel and catering industry, in clubs, on licenced premises and in domestic service are typical of jobs requiring married couples or partners. If the job entails company or business entertaining, they may wish to see how you and your partner react in this type of situation. If it is also an overseas appointment of some importance to the company, then the commitment of your partner to living overseas may be a critical factor in the final decision-making process.

Shortcomings of the interview

Despite its potential benefits, the interview as an assessment method has been criticized for more than seventy years. It is considered only a modest predictor of job performance because of its low levels of reliability and validity. An assessment technique is considered reliable if different interviewers using it at the same time on the same people give them the same ratings. Validity is concerned with the extent to which the technique actually predicts what it is supposed to predict and not something else, i.e. 'Will this person achieve the results we want if we appoint them?'

Most research studies come to the conclusion that, rather than using interviews, organizations would probably be better off selecting people by 'tossing a coin'. However, it would probably be true to say that the problems are with the interviewers and the way in which they conduct interviews rather than the method itself. The interview is a conversation with a purpose and is only as good as the people who use it. Some of the many criticisms levelled at interviewers suggest that they tend to:

- give undue weight to their initial contact with candidates and a higher overall assessment to candidates who are interpersonally attractive, even though this may not be critical for job performance: the 'first impressions' error;
- have their decisions influenced by the quality of preceding candidates: the 'contrast effect';

- rate more highly those candidates whom they believe are in some way(s) like themselves and where one piece of favourable information contaminates everything else favourably: the 'Halo' effect;
- treat it as a search for negative information and where one unfavourable piece of information contaminates everything else negatively and leads to rejection: the 'Horn' effect;
- give different weight of importance to the same information, over-value academic qualifications and give unfavourable information more weight than any other;
- compare and contrast candidates one against the other rather than the personnel specification and then change their stereotype of the 'ideal' candidate as the interview progresses.

These are NOT invariable behaviours of all interviewers or criticisms of all interviews. They are comments which have been revealed by numerous small-scale research studies over many years. Some of these will undoubtedly apply to the interviews you attend. Thus they throw a great deal of onus on you to impress your interviewers favourably from the outset.

Over the years ways have been sought to improve the interview rather than to dispense with it. These are being achieved by better training and using more structured interviews which produce better predictions of job performance. Further improvements are obtained when interviewers concentrate more on job-related questions such as work experience, training and interest. Some research suggests that the use of an interviewing panel may also improve the validity of an interview when a less structured, biographical approach is used but *not* when a more structured format is followed. Predictions are improved by supplementing the interview with other techniques such as extended selection procedures and Multiple Assessment Centres.

The day of your interview

At last the day arrives. You may be travelling on the day of your interview or on the previous day. Attendance at an extended selection procedure or Multiple Assessment Centre often requires you to arrive at the venue the previous evening. If so, be prepared for activities such as a battery of psychological tests or company presentation(s). There may also be a formal meal with managers (and for graduate recruitment there may be some of last year's intake available for informal discussions). If you are invited to this type of 'socialising' beforehand, then be aware that you are being assessed. They will not expect you to use the wrong cutlery, drink to excess, insult everyone when you have had too much, be ill because of your over-indulgence, forget the common courtesies of a guest and turn up to dinner in a T-shirt, jeans and trainers.

Sometimes the 'dirty tricks' brigade operate during extended selection procedures or Assessment Centres. This may well not be deliberate but the situation provides potential 'traps' into which the unwary can fall. An assessor may well try to provoke you during what appears to be an informal, across-the-table discussion. Be wary of making extreme comments in unguarded moments. And there may be panel members who have hollow legs. Don't try to keep up with their liquid intake. It's OK if they go to sleep during the interview but not so good if you can't coordinate your lips and your brain when being questioned.

Whether your invitation is to an extended selection procedure or an interview, you should remember the following.

Pre-interview checklist

- Have with you all correspondence you need and anything they asked you to bring.
- Take something to write with and on.
- Take a spare copy of your CV.
- Take a Phonecard and small change for parking or phone calls.
- Check your itinerary and timings.
- Check your passport, currency, tickets (and phrase book?) if travelling overseas.
- Plan what you are going to wear and lay out your clothes the previous evening.
- Pack your bag with overnight clothes and toiletries, etc.
- Clean your shoes the night before.
- Do your 'last minute' revision.

There are other points worth considering:

Try to get your normal night's sleep beforehand. Some people suggest 'get a good night's sleep' – whatever that means. My advice is not to do anything too far away from your normal evening habits Your body will be expecting what it normally gets. A 'good night's sleep' for one person is deprivation for another.

Eat normally. Some people advise you to 'eat a good or hearty breakfast'. It sounds like the advice for the proverbial 'condemned man'. I would suggest you do what you normally do. Your digestive system is accustomed to a particular diet and you should stick to that. If you are abroad, don't go mad at the breakfast self-service counter and stay away from the garlic and strong smelling concoctions. Interviewers don't usually appreciate being accosted by heavily aromatic breath.

As well as not eating strong-smelling dishes beforehand, do **not** fortify yourself with liquid 'Dutch courage'. A breathy 'How do you do?' laced with spirits when being introduced to the interviewers does not go down well.

Martin was an ex-merchant marine engineer in his late thirties. He had found his 'shore legs' more than a year ago and had still not managed to obtain employment. Whilst he undoubtedly had a lot to offer suitable employers, he was unable to package and present his transferable skills in an acceptable way. His level of frustration was so great that, he told me, he had actually torn telephone handsets off the walls of telephone booths when trying to get appointments for interviews. We reviewed his approach and he revealed that, because interviews made him so nervous, he needed a couple of 'doubles' before he went in. We weaned him away from that dubious practice and helped him develop his self-assessment and presentation skills. About five weeks after the training programme and counselling he roared up to my office on his motorcycle and asked me to sit down with him and help him decide which offer he should choose from the three in his hand.

A final piece of advice you might be given is to arrive between five and ten minutes before your appointed time. A fun way of looking at this might be the comments of some psychologists that: 'The high-anxiety type arrives early, the obsessional will arrive bang on time and the self-confident, arrogant extrovert arrives late, sweaty, out of breath and having upset everyone in the organization they have met on the way to the interview room.'

What should you do about time? Easy. Use the normal, logical approach to achieving anything on time. Plan backwards from the time your invitation states you have to be there. Build in sufficient time to do whatever you think necessary from the checklist.

Your arrival checklist

- Find the place.
- Park your car (if you have one) and pay the fee/get a ticket.
- Walk to the 'gate' or reception.
- Sign in and get a badge.
- See about expenses where appropriate.
- Walk to the interview location, e.g. a waiting room which might be some distance away from your point of arrival.
- Find out a little 'intelligence' about the interviewing arrangements such as number of candidates, duration, etc.
- Visit the washroom to freshen up and go to the toilet.
- Change your shirt/blouse if you are anxious or it is very humid and you perspire readily.
- Clean your shoes, tidy your appearance, brush your hair.
- Compose yourself, sit quietly and browse through your documents or any company literature lying around.
- Do your deep breathing or relaxation exercises, repeat your Mantra or whatever your guru suggests.
- See if you can get yourself a cup of tea or coffee or something to help you relax and clear your throat.
- If you need to smoke, then make sure you are directed to an official smoking area.
- Engage in pleasantries with the people in reception –

they may be part of the informal assessment procedure. (Always behave pleasantly towards any level of the organization's employee you meet. It costs nothing and could be worth a lot.)

If you can do what you feel you ought to in five to ten minutes, so be it. But remember, the interviewers can afford to be running late – you can't. And they may even be running early because some thoughtless candidate has forgotten to tell them that they are not coming at all or are going to be late.

When you arrive there may be a waiting area where you report or you may be taken along to a one nearer the interviewing room. These could range from a relatively bare room or corridor through a whole variety up to a thickly carpeted anteroom with comfortable furniture, pleasant furnishings, potted plants, fish tanks, magazines, newspapers and copies of the company's in-house journals or annual reports strewn invitingly around. Other candidates may be waiting either to go in or who have already been interviewed and have been asked to remain behind until the last interview is completed.

Be observant about and sensitive to what you see around you as you walk through the building(s) to get to the interviewing room. What impressions are you getting physically, socially and psychologically? What are the fixtures, fittings and furnishings like? How well maintained and cleaned are the areas you walk through? What signs of status are there in the environment and on the people? How do the staff treat you? Is there an air of shabbiness or overdone opulence? How busy do the employees seem? What is the technology like? You may be asked to comment on any of these. Some interviewers could have as one of their own special questions something to do with your 'first impressions' of them.

The interview environment

Interviewing rooms vary considerably. They could be the corner of a lounge in a hotel or a bedroom which has had the beds taken out; space behind screens in an open-plan area; an office varying from the size of a tablecloth to one so large that there are several metres of emptiness or tables between you and the interviewer(s). In local government and educational establishments interviews may be held in some large, imposing, oak-panelled, official function chamber. It may also be a screened-off area in a large hall or gymnasium. (I have even had to interview school leavers in a large stationery cupboard with no windows!)

You may well talk more quietly if over-awed by your surroundings or when in a large room. Make allowances for this and ensure the interviewers can hear you. There is an unfortunate tendency for some people to become more formal when being interviewed in formal surroundings. Skilled and sensitive interviewers ought to know better. On the one hand they probably wish you to relax a little. On the other hand formal environments bring out formal behaviours. The opposite also is true: smaller, more intimate settings encourage self-revelation. Be careful that you do not become over-relaxed and 'spill the beans' or become too 'buddy-buddy'. Some older, more mature women trying to get back to work after having raised a family may fall into the trap of thinking that the interview is a cosy tête-à-tête – especially if the interviewers are also women. It is a business meeting and should be treated in that way.

Some interviewers will wish to create a more informal environment to try to reduce your anxieties and make you feel comfortable. They might succeed. On the other hand, some organizations – the more status-conscious bureaucracies – will wish to emphasize their superiority, enhance their image, maintain their social distance – and still want you to speak and behave more or less normally and be prepared to exchange confidences. Arrangements should have been made for privacy: no ringing telephones, chattering printers, buzzing fax machines or heads poking around the door asking: 'When will you be finished with that one?'

The furniture in the room will also vary greatly. With a bit of luck there will be somewhere for you to hang your outer garments and place your other impedimenta – umbrella, document or briefcase, overnight bag, etc. You may find yourself in the corner of a large office seated on an easy chair with a low coffee table between you and the interviewer. For women with short skirts this could be somewhat disconcerting – constantly trying to feel comfortable in such a situation. (Or perhaps it will be the interviewer who doesn't know where to look.) Ordinary office chairs may have been placed across the corner of a table or on opposing sides of an office desk. In the most extreme cases you will be asked to sit on a seat isolated from the panel, who may be ranged around you on two or three sides. This could well feel rather like a contemporary version of 'When did you last see your father?' – more of an inquisition than an interview. You must also recognize that some interviewers are only comfortable if there is a physical space or barrier between them and the candidates. A desk gives them the comfort and protection they feel they need.

The seating arrangement most often recommended during interviewer training programmes is for as many physical barriers as possible to be removed, i.e. no large spaces or tables between interviewers and interviewees. Some interviewing arrangements preclude this. If there are panels of up to 12 or more people it becomes a little difficult to create an environment for an intimate conversation.

The 'dirty tricks' brigade

The mythology of interviews tells us that the 'dirty tricks' brigade will sit you on a lower chair than theirs with one leg shorter than the rest and facing into the sun. If it happens, what do you do? It's probably better not to sit and squint uncomfortably, shade your eyes with your hands, get out your sunglasses and put them on or move your chair into a more shaded position. Ask, calmly, if you can re-position your chair so that the glare isn't affecting you. It's difficult to know whether such interviewers are deliberately trying to create situations or they merely lack social sensitivity and basic interpersonal courtesies? Whichever it is, it's all part of your assessment of them.

They may also point you in the direction of two chairs on 'your' side of the table so that you have to make a choice. Just sit in whichever you think is most comfortable and convenient.

Another ploy is for the interviewer suddenly to stand up and ask you to come around to his side of the table and say: 'I want you to sit in my chair and interview me for this job.' I heard of one candidate who sat down, buzzed through for the secretary and ordered two coffees before he started the 'mock' interview.

Then there is the old trick of: 'What's the name of the house magazine on the table outside?' or 'How many chairs/pictures are there in the waiting room? (People who are compulsive 'counters' probably score high on this one.)

If these sort of dubious practices are in evidence and you feel that this is not the job or organization for you, try what one psychologist is reputed to have done. Halfway through the interview he jumped up from his seat, placed his hand on the small of his back and then lay down in the middle of the room saying, 'Please carry on. I have this occasional twinge in the sacro-iliac area and I just have to stretch out flat.' Apparently the effect on the interviewer was a delight to see. The interview was terminated and the psychologist felt that he had won – even though he was not offered the job.

Try not to be intimidated by whatever arrangements confront you. You should always try to find out when you arrive what the actual interviewing room is like – if only to reduce a natural fear of the unknown.

Face-to-face at last

Whilst interviewers seem to have their personal preferences, procedures and practices, there are some common factors. I shall describe a very conventional approach which tends to reflect what many interviewers do, what is found in some text books on interviewing and what is taught on some selection interviewing courses. Variations will be introduced as we proceed.

■ *How long might an interview last?*

How long is a piece of string? They might range from fifteen minutes to more than an hour – even if they are only 'screening' interviews. A final interview could stretch up to two hours. There is no recommended standard. They ought to last as long as it takes to achieve their purpose. A panel interview may take no longer than a one-to-one. Sometimes you will get an indication of the duration from the invitation. You may be able to ask at the Reception if they have a copy of the interviewing timetable to check off the candidates as they arrive. Sometimes it will be mentioned at the start of the interview.

■ *Number of interviewers*

This varies. It could be a single one-to-one situation or several one-to-one interviews with different people 'in series', e.g. someone from Personnel, followed by the Manager with the vacancy, moving on to a specialist in your field and finishing with a more senior person – Departmental or Divisional Manager, Director, Managing Director, Chief Executive or Chairman. It all depends on the job for which you are being considered.

At the other extreme, you may be faced by a panel which could increase in numbers from two people up to double figures. One manager told me that at one local government interview he attended there were as many as 40 people on the panel. I have experienced a dozen myself. More recently I have had confirmation that up to ten is not uncommon for local government and similar appointments.

On some panels there may be specialist or co-opted members. They will take a very specific role as the expert adviser to the interviewers or the organization. They may or may not be from inside the organization. Their assessment will be very important when the final decisions are being made. Make sure you give them your best attention and 'good' answers. This strategy is more often used in local government, academic and scientific appointments, but it may also be used by smaller organizations making their first specialist or functional appointment. The 'quiet one' at the end of the row may also be a psychologist or specialist in observing body language.

Whenever you are confronted by a panel you should especially:

- make eye contact with and listen attentively to the person asking the question,
- reply to the questioner and make eye contact as you do,
- if in doubt, go back to the person in the 'Chair',
- try to answer one question at a time.

Some panels are very badly organized. You may experience the following:

- you won't be introduced to anyone,
- you are introduced to everyone so quickly you forget who they are,
- they won't have name plates in front of them so you won't know who they are when they speak to you,
- they have not decided who is going to cover which aspects of you and your experiences,

- they argue amongst themselves about the questions and the answers,
- they interrupt you and each other,
- they disagree about the work and the conditions of employment,
- some will read papers, stare out of the window and feign sleep.

For some appointments the Personnel Department have a great deal of influence. They may conduct the interviews and make offers of employment. In other situations they may have minimal involvement. All actions after advertising or shortlisting have taken place may be done by the employing manager. This is especially true in geographically-dispersed organizations. Regional and branch managers often have total control over the recruitment and selection process and the final interviews.

The professional view is that, whenever feasible, the person to whom you report should exercise a great deal of influence in the final decision. After all, that is the person for whom you are going to work and a manager is only as good as the people who work for him. Their success depends on their ability to select people. The less they are involved, the greater the likelihood that they will blame someone else for the quality of their staff. Obviously this philosophy is more difficult, if not impossible, to apply if you are being recruited for Police and Armed Forces and some graduate and trainee appointments. This doesn't mean you should only concentrate upon pleasing the ultimate 'consumer' of your skills. Other people will have varying levels of influence on the final decision. Give of your best at every interview. This can be a bit of a chore when you have a succession or series of individual interviews with people who seem to be covering the same ground. Imagine what it must be like in some countries where as many as six interviews is not unknown before you are finally offered employment? Try to avoid saying 'I've already told that to the previous interviewers.' Your performance and attitudes must improve on the telling and not deteriorate.

■ *The interview sequence*

There are two ends to the interview sequence spectrum. At one extreme they will be totally unstructured because the interviewers feel that suits them best or because they don't know any better. At the other extreme they will be highly structured because that is the method the interviewers have been taught and which is favoured by the organization. In between there will be a form of structure or sequence suggested to or used by interviewers which could be something like the following, generalized and logical approach followed by many interviewers from the outset:

Opening

Smile
Greeting
Relieve you of your coat, umbrella, briefcase, etc
Handshake
Use your name (to make sure they have the right person in front of them)
Introduce everyone
Sit you down comfortably
Offer you refreshments if appropriate
Mention the title of the vacancy (people have been known to be in front of the wrong interviewers when several interviews are running in parallel in adjacent rooms)
Exchange pleasantries or break the ice with 'small talk' such as weather, travel, etc (but not for too long)
Tell you they will be taking notes
Describe their interview approach such as:

- information from you
- job details later
- answering your questions at the end

Once the interviewers have covered these formalities – sometimes by glancing at their own checklists – they will wish to get you talking. If there are two or more people, the chairperson will probably tell you who is going to ask about what and either start by questioning you or passing you on to the first interviewer.

There are several possible approaches to the start of an interview. They can begin by telling you something about the job or they might leave this to the end. Both of these options have advantages and disadvantages for you and the organization. If you have been forewarned about the job in the information pack then you will certainly be expected to answer quite probing questions about the organization and the work. You should also have some pertinent questions to ask them. If you already know something about the work or it is described to you in any depth at the start of the interview, and you are reasonably bright, you will be able to align your experiences to fit the job as described. You emphasize those aspects of your track record which are requirements for success in their job.

If you haven't found anything out about the job or organization, don't ask them initially unless invited to do so. By doing this you may be admitting lack of preparation and low interest in the appointment. Some interviewers will not provide you with job information until the end. They may even expect you to take a pro-active approach and ask them questions. Alternatively they might describe the job or even give you a short description of the job for you to read and ask questions about. If you are not going to be provided with information about the job until the end, then one tactic used by interviewers is to ask you what you think the work entails early on in the interview. This checks on your preparation and your perceptions. Lack of preparation and inaccurate perceptions may be sound reasons for probing you strongly or just rejecting you as unsuitable for the post.

Exploring

There are a number of ways in which the main body of the interview could proceed.

There is the vacuum technique, which is probably more appropriate if you are intelligent and with lengthy or varied experiences. It is rather like giving you a length of rope when you enter the room and seeing how quickly you hang yourself. The interviewer may start off with something like:

'Tell me about yourself.'
'Give me a brief history of your life since leaving full-time education.'
'Tell me about your work experiences.'

They create the vacuum and leave you to fill it. You could always try asking them what they would like you to cover. The more skilled might then say:

'Just leave it to you . . . get you talking before I start asking you questions.'

This could be a golden opportunity for you to make a good first impression by highlighting your strengths in relation to their appointment during a quick résumé of your career to date. They often just sit and listen without comment or question – possibly making occasional notes of something to talk about later on. If you go quiet, they may just sit there and look at you, waiting for you to continue – the 'silent' treatment.

Another approach, if you are younger with little or no work experience, would be for them to start with your educational or academic circumstances and work around these with questions such as:

'Tell me about your school.'
'Describe a typical weekend.'
'What's your favourite hobby/pastime?'
'Do you do any work on Saturdays or during the holidays?'
'What's your best subject at school?'
'Are you in any clubs or societies?'
'Tell me about where you go on holiday.'

If you have a lengthy work history, then they may ask you to start with your latest appointment and work backwards. An obvious variation on this for people with less work experience is to start with the first full-time job and work chronologically up to date. The older you are and the longer your track record, the more likely the interviewer's emphasis will eventually be on your more recent appointments and those which bear the greatest relevance to their vacancy.

Many interviewers will have been trained to go through your application form or conduct a biographical interview. This means going through each of your work experiences to explore the two main aspects of any interview: the extent to which you can do the work and what you are like as a person. They may cover your work experiences by asking about:

How many jobs you have had.
Their dates.
With whom and doing what.
Why you chose that company and that type of work.
What training you received.
What you learned and contributed with them.
Any progression you may have had.
Your responsibilities.

The things you liked and disliked about the work and the company.
Your reasons for changing/wanting to change.
How you related to other people.
Leadership experiences where appropriate.
Their 'test' or technical questions related to the job content.

This approach could be somewhat repetitive since they might wish to have answers to the above questions for all your jobs – or certainly those which are most relevant to their needs.

They might then move on to:

Your interests outside work.
Education and qualifications if these have not been covered earlier.
Domestic circumstances in relation to mobility, travel, etc.
Attendance records and state of health.
Your aspirations and how their appointment fits in with these.

If you have done your preparation you ought to have little difficulty in coping with this part of the interview. What you need to look out for are signs that they are getting towards the end of their exploration. Their questions may become shorter. They may stop asking for further information. Their body language may indicate that it is time for you to go. They will move you towards the final phase.

Closing

Towards the end of the interview you may be told something about the job and the organization – its products, services, future plans, philosophies. If you have already received a lot of information, they may turn the tables and ask you questions like:

What you think of the job?
Why you are interested in it?
Why you applied?
In what ways it is better than your present post?

They may also expect you to ask questions rather than be spoon-fed with more information. This is the point where you could be invited to ask any questions you may have about the work or the organization. Useful questions for you to ask could cover the following if they have not been made clear in any prior correspondence or during the interview:

Induction.
Training.
Company support for further education.
Whom you will report to directly.
What happened to the last incumbent.
What are the prospects like.
In what ways is the organization changing over the next few years.
When can you expect a decision.
When they would you like you to start.
What about holidays you have already reserved.

You should note these on a slip of paper and refer to them when the time comes. It indicates that you have thought about the organization and the job, but don't make a big thing of it. It is probably better not to raise the question of salary at this point unless they do. It depends on how clear the 'benefits package' is in the information you have already had. Perhaps 'Could you tell me how the total salary and benefits package is put together?' might be an acceptable approach. If incentive, bonus or commission schemes are part of the package, it would be useful to discuss these – but don't give the impression that this is your main concern. You should wish to know about how you participate, what standards are set, how you would be assessed, what the payments are, what tax liabilities are attracted, what form the incentive takes, etc.

After they have answered your questions they could go on to talk about:

Medicals.
References.
Your availability if offered the job.
Any firm holiday commitments you might have.
What happens next in the procedure.

They may also ask you something like:

'Is there anything you would like to say finally in support of your application?'
'Is there anything I haven't asked you which you thought I might?'
'Is there anything else you would like to tell me about yourself?'

These may present you with your last opportunity to shine. But be careful that you don't put your foot in it. Look out for signals from the interviewer(s) that they want things to come to a close such as:

Yawning.
Looking out of the window.
Shuffling with papers – especially tidying them up.
Writing notes and not taking much notice of what you are saying.
Glaring at you and not smiling.
Staring at the clock on the wall.
Looking at their watches.
Listening to their watches.
Taking off their watches and banging them on the table.
Getting up from their chairs to 'stretch a leg'.
Interrupting your flow of words.
Holding out an arm with their palm facing towards you.

They may ask about your expenses. Have your calculations ready. I believe these are best dealt with outside of the interview with the receptionist or secretary. Your invitation should have indicated what their practice is. You may be able to submit a claim afterwards.

You should end by shaking hands and thanking them by name for their time. Some organizations may invite you to have a 'tour' of the premises. If you feel it appropriate, you could always ask if a quick 'walkabout' would be possible. It might underline your interest.

After some interviews you may be asked to wait to be told the outcome, i.e. whether or not you are to be offered the appointment or who has been selected. This is not unusual for local government or educational appointments. Occasionally you will be told not to stay and that you will be contacted – sometimes that evening by telephone – and told of the result, which will later be confirmed in writing. More often you will just be told that you will 'Hear within the next 'x' days.'

■ *What do the interviewers do afterwards?*

You have played your part – for better or for worse – and your career is now in their hands.

Immediately afterwards the interviewers should tidy up any additional information they obtained from you, search for the 'fit' between your track record and the job experiences they require and check your facts and their impressions against other sources, evidence and people. All of their information should be interpreted by comparing you and the other candidates against the personnel specification and not against each other.

They should record their impressions and recommendations on your suitability, often by using an assessment form. They must identify those qualities which will help you to succeed at the job and ask of things which might hinder your job performance: 'Can they be changed by training and development?'

If possible they will select the person most likely to succeed and choose an acceptable runner up if there is one. If there really are no suitable candidates then they ought not to pick a 'second best' and rationalize their choice – usually by changing the personnel specification to fit the 'best' person they saw. They will usually initiate employment administration such as arranging for medicals, references, security clearance and for offers of appointment, etc to go suitable applicants. Finally, they should have a good 'Public Relations' rejection letter sent to unsuccessful applicants and write a pleasant but business-like letter to those who have to be rejected once the first choice accepts the appointment.

These are idealized practices. In real life interviewers may make their final decision as soon as you enter the room, during the interview or as soon as you leave. They may change their 'ideal' person profile to fit the 'best' candidate they have interviewed or decide to alter the job requirements for the same reason. Often they will hurry off to their next appointment and possibly get together with other interviewers at a later date to make their decision when they have forgotten who you are.

The final thing a thoughtful organization will do is continually to review its recruitment and selection procedures to ensure that they are cost-beneficial. This may mean keeping records on response rates to different resourcing methods and the costs incurred in these. They should also record the interview results, which may be needed for use in any Industrial Tribunals or appeals arising from complaints of unfair or discriminatory practices. A professional organization will follow up the people selected to check on their attendance, performance, relationships, satisfaction, potential, progress and suitability. The purpose of all of these activities is to improve the skills of those involved throughout the recruitment process – and especially of those who make the final selection decisions. Unfortunately there is little evidence that these types of activity are conscientiously undertaken by all organizations.

Despite all of the preparation done by some organizations, the final decision could well be purely subjective. You may be chosen or rejected on the grounds of 'interpersonal chemistry', i.e. 'Could I work with this person?'

Screening interviews

Shortlisting or 'screening' interviews are not uncommon for appointments at all levels – from retail assistant and undergraduates through to more senior appointments where there are dozens of applicants or where an external agency is undertaking the first 'sift' for the organization.

It may be apparent from the invitation that you are being asked to attend a 'preliminary discussion'. Treat this as seriously as if it was the final interview. If you do badly it certainly will be your last interview as you won't reach the finals. You must do as much preparation as you can. Often its purpose is to obtain a quick 'first impression' which is especially important in appointments where dealing with the public is a critical requirement for job success – and usually you will only have between 20 and 30 minutes to do it. However, some shortlisting procedures may also require you to undertake a written exercise and one or two psychological tests at this stage. The results both of the interview and the tests will be taken into account when the organization makes the decision whether or not to allow you to continue.

Pay particular attention to your dress and appearance. Smile, make eye contact, shake hands firmly, be on your 'best behaviour' and try to project some warmth and enthusiasm through your body language. Discover something about the way the organization operates and have some questions ready to ask the interviewers. All of these tactics will help to demonstrate your interest. Say that you would be only too pleased to attend for a further discussion. Coverage of your job experience will often be superficial at this stage. You should still be able to highlight where your experience and their requirements match.

A typical approach used for a university 'milk round' interview could include:

1 Introduction of them, you, their purpose and procedure and how long the interview will last.

2 A settling-in phase where you will be encouraged to talk about yourself – possibly using an interest, hobby or outstanding achievement as your starter.

3 The main body of the interview, during which they will wish to pursue your personal and educational development, your intellectual ability and your career motivation. The types of questions could cover things like:

'Why have you chosen this college/course of study?'
'How is it going and what do you expect to obtain?'
'How do you feel about yourself?'
'How would you like to use your degree studies?'
'What would you say is the most difficult situation you have ever had to deal with?'
'Why are you interested in working for us?'

Your intellectual ability may be tested by a hypothetical situation with which you may or may not be familiar.

4 Any questions you may wish to ask.

5 Closing remarks related to the next stage in the procedure and when you are likely to hear from them.

If you have only about 30 minutes and they see several people each day for several days over several weeks, they are going to set their sights very high and rely to an inordinate amount on their first impressions of you and your ability to get into top gear quite quickly. My personal feeling is that, other things being equal such as basic academic qualifications, interviewers would be advised to select the undergraduate who can tell them more about their organization during this first interview. At least they have shown an interest in and bothered to prepare for the meeting. The university 'milk round' still appears to be popular with many organizations who may not yet have undertaken cost-benefit analyses of this method or explored more effective and efficient alternatives.

Stress interviews

Just as 'Beauty is in the eye of the beholder' then stress and stress interviews may come into the same category. What one person would perceive as a stress interview or a stressful situation, another might respond to as a challenge. It is probably not a common and deliberate practice for organizations and interviewers to use stress interviews for selecting staff.

Michael had always felt disadvantaged by not having a degree. Many of his peers had gone through a university education and he still occasionally met some of them. Colleagues at work were graduates and a large number of the other staff were well qualified. He was interested in becoming a salesman and replied to an advert placed in the local press by a national company. It was the usual sales advertisement: '. . . no experience needed, training given . . .' and no mention of qualifications being required. He attended an interview in the local office and was told by the manager that his application would be passed on to the next stage. Shortly afterwards he was invited to a second interview in a northern city some 100 miles away. This meant a day off work and another 'funeral to attend'. The regional manager interviewed him and said that he was going to be recommended for a further interview in London with the national sales manager. No mention of lack of experience or qualifications had been made in either interview so far. Another invitation arrived for an interview in the London. Another day off work – sick? He disliked all of this subterfuge but there was no other way. He arrived in London by the earliest train and made his way to the company's sales HQ. The building was old, prison-like and resembled a rabbit warren. The doorman gave him sufficient instructions and he ended up outside the interview room, sitting on the cold stone steps of a spiral staircase – waiting to go in. The interview was running late and Michael was concerned about his rather tight journey timings. Finally he was called into a bare, cell-like room with a table and two chairs, one on either side of the table. The interview progressed in the way of all interviews with the interviewer occasionally asking about Michael's lack of sales experience, qualifications and further education. Every now and then he would come back to: 'Of course you haven't got any higher qualifications'. The trigger which fired Michael's gun was: 'Well, of course you haven't got any qualifications and we normally employ graduates to do this work.' Michael's response was like the crack of a rifle: 'Listen mate, if I had a degree I certainly wouldn't want to go around the country hawking your margarine.' That seemed to bring the interview to an end. At least Michael got his expenses – eventually.

It is obviously easier to create stress for some people than others. You may be the sort of person who carries a lot of natural anxiety around with you. It may well be brought to the surface in a strange environment or in situations where there is a lot at stake – especially questions of ego-involvement and pressure on your self-image. If interviewers wish to create a stressful situation deliberately then they would undertake as many of the following as they could.

The stress interview

Stress may be created if interviewers:

- keep you waiting
- in an uncomfortable ante-room
- with no one else there
- use a large, impersonal interviewing area
- with physical and spacial barriers between you and the interviewers – large tables for them and only a small chair for you
- formal seating arrangement in which you are
- outnumbered by at least 5 to 1 and subject to
- cursory and rapid introductions – if any at all
- straight down to antagonistic or provocative questions and statements such as:

  'You seem to be a bit of a job hopper.'

  'Do you always dress like that?'

  'What makes you think you could do this job?'
- using quick-fire questioning
- from random interviewers
- in no logical sequence
- which they don't allow you to answer fully because of
- continual interruptions
- accompanied by domineering body language
- with aggressive probing and challenging

Using such tactics in a threatening environment will elicit abnormal behaviour. Exactly what game the interviewers are playing and why is hard to know. But many of the above tactics feature in what some interviewers would describe as 'our normal practice'. Whilst working with one Police Force introducing some of their middle management uniformed officers to selection interviewing, I was asked to teach them the 'hard man, soft man' approach. I quickly commented on the unsuitability of that technique for selection purposes.

What might be happening that you could perceive as being stressful? The mere thought of having to be questioned by one or more persons, the outcome of which will affect your life, may well be extremely stressful enough for you. If the interviewers then deliberately amplify your concerns in a number of ways, you will certainly feel stressed.

How will you cope with a stress interview? Careful preparation will help. Stay in Adult. Don't let your Child state get 'hooked'. Discussing their approach or even confronting them with it might make the interviewers sit up. Perhaps they don't know what they are doing. You could always decide to 'take it further' – initially to the top of the organization, or perhaps with the Institute of Personnel Management or the local press if you feel you have been treated unfairly. Thoughtless and unprofessional use of this technique tends to break the third caveat of the selection interview: that it should also be a good PR activity.

Structured interviews

The biographical and screening approaches described earlier have a structure. More tightly structured formats are used by organizations who feel they are more appropriate for selecting employees below professional and managerial levels. This could be for appointments where there are many people doing identical work and the costs of developing and using structured interviews are spread over more appointments.

Several approaches have been developed, usually after very thorough job analyses. Research indicates that these can improve interview validity under certain circumstances. They tend, however, to be very constraining for interviewers used to a biographical approach. As a candidate you might not find them too boring. As an interviewer doing several each day it could lead to intellectual constipation. Compared with less structured formats, they have been found to be beneficial in a number of ways. They reduce the weight given to first impressions and candidate attractiveness when all candidates have to undertake simulations or use job materials. Job relevance becomes more potent when interviewers are making their final assessments and choices. Coverage is more consistent between and within candidates and suitability ratings are more reliable. Interviewers talk less and candidates talk more. Validity is therefore increased.

One structured approach is somewhat like the biographical interview except that the interviewers have a long list of pre-determined questions. Beside each is a space for them to note your answers (and sometimes what should be inferred from your responses). The interviewers go through this same sequence with every candidate. When they have interviewed everyone they review what has been collected and make their final assessment and decision. This could well come across as being very stilted if it does not allow the interviewer to probe you. The disadvantage for you is that there could be little scope for you to inject information if the 'right' questions are not being asked. The advantage for the organization is that the interviewers exercise total control and the procedure becomes a true test or examination: all candidates are asked the same questions in the same sequence. It is also much easier for the interviewers to 'score' responses, reduce subjectivity and improve reliability.

The **situational interview** can be used where job analysis reveals specific critical behaviours for successful job performance from which a sample of work-related situations is developed. The interview then concentrates on what you would do in each of these hypothetical situations. This is a very structured procedure which permits all candidates to be scored more objectively. But it is also open to good theoretical answers unrelated to what you might do when faced with the real situation. What people say is not necessarily what they do. Actions speak louder than words.

This objection can be overcome by using the **behaviour description interview** which is based on the premise that the best guide to what someone will do in the future is what they have done in the past. Job analysis reveals critical activities which can be translated into specific, standard questions beginning with:

'Tell me about a time when you . . .'

The shortcoming is that not everyone may have had the required experience(s). Thus different questions may have to be put to each candidate according to their unique background and experience – or lack of it. Under these circumstances it becomes difficult to score and assess candidates objectively. (It might highlight training needs provided the person has the aptitude for and desire to do the work.) However, follow-up studies of this type of interview have shown a useful correlation with job performance.

A variation on this is the **patterned behaviour description interview**. The interviewers will explore your reasons for making the various changes in your life. They build up a longitudinal picture of your past from which they predict your likely reactions to future changes and the directions in which you would wish your career to take. They then match their findings with what they know to be the likely changes in the appointment for which you are being considered. An increasing amount of information is available about career patterns derived from biographical analyses of work experiences, the inference being that the past portends the future.

Another approach is the **comprehensive structured interview** covering situational, job knowledge, job simulation and worker requirements. The situational area explores your previous job experience in broad terms. Under the job knowledge category you would be asked hypothetical questions about critical job areas, e.g. 'What would you do if you had to . . . ?' Under the job simulation category you would be asked to actually do something required of the job holder. That might mean, for instance, dealing with a disciplinary interview role play, completing an 'In-Tray' exercise, role-playing a conversation with an angry customer or in a telephone sales situation, or making, shaping or assembling something or driving a vehicle. The final area of worker requirements would be exploring your attitudes and behaviours by asking you to comment on situations, e.g. 'You will have to . . . Tell us how you feel about that?'

This technique is more comprehensive than the others and requires a very structured scoring guide for the interviewers to ensure objectivity and reliability.

A rigorous approach is used by the Post Office for graduate, managerial and professional selection. Post Office staff trained in this approach may also use it for selecting other grades of employee and for internal promotions. It is based on a number of essential dimensions to be explored with candidates in separate interviews. The selection procedure takes the form of a one-day assessment centre. You undertake combinations of the following activities in addition to at least three separate interviews:

- psychological instruments covering ability, personality and occupational interests.
- an 'In-tray' exercise.
- individual business proposal case study which might then be discussed amongst the candidates (between four and six of you) or presented to the interviewers.
- a group discussion or individual presentation requiring individual preparation.

The two, structured, one-to-one discussions are referred to as the Personnel Assessor (PA) and the Operational Assessor (OA) interviews and each last about one hour. You would also be interviewed by the chairperson of that particular assessment centre. (In addition, for some assessment centres, there may also be another separate interview with an occupational psychologist who discusses with the candidates the results and implications of their psychological tests and questionnaires.)

The Personnel Assessor would be concerned with finding out what you have done and how you feel about your life in terms of your purposefulness, resilience, interpersonal skills and maturity. These are considered important dimensions for graduate entrants (and undoubtedly for other appointments). They are explored using a more or less biographical approach based on careful analysis of your application form. Questioning will largely be concerned with your responsibilities, occasions where you have succeeded and failed, your attitudes towards people and events and how you have dealt with difficulties and pressure situations. The concern is with what you have done and not with hypothetical situations.

The Operational Assessor is concerned with establishing your ability to use your imagination, make practical judgements and apply your intellect. Thus the OA is concerned with how you might deal with situations rather than how you have dealt with things in the past. This is complementary to the work of the PA. The OA pursues these areas by getting you to talk around three topics. One is likely to be a subject nominated by you on your application form. Alternatively, it might be a topic which the interviewer has extracted from your application form as being something with which you are familiar. Another topic will be a subject with which you have no experience whatsoever, such as a problem or something of interest to the organization and which you may have to face if you join them. The third topic could be one which you may or may not know anything about. In all three instances the assessor will set the scene, ask you to produce ideas and thoughts on the subject which are beyond the everyday and orthodox, see whether or not you can put forward a logical case to support your ideas, defend them if necessary, show how they might be applied practically and where they could possibly fall down, what you might do to cope with such eventualities or in situations where sudden, unexpected constraints are thrown at you. In other words, this is a test of your ability to 'think on your feet' in areas outside of your normal experience.

Relatively few organizations use the structured techniques described above. It is unlikely that you will be aware of their interview format beforehand – unless you are able to talk to someone in the organization, a colleague or an acquaintance who has been through the selection procedure.

Many trained interviewers tend to follow a biographical approach and this is probably the tactic for which you should prepare yourself. It forms a sound basis for responding sensibly under any of the other formats – except the hypothetical ones – which require you to 'think on your seat'.

Telephone interviews

Some advertisements may ask you to 'telephone for further details or an application form, etc'. This may be a ploy to give you a 'mini' interview over the phone. Organizations which do this may have discovered a number of critical personal attributes which discriminate between more and less successful applicants and can be determined during a structured telephone conversation. Their questions will possibly be aimed at deterring you if you appear to be an unsuitable applicant. Do some 'homework' before you pick up the phone – or at least be prepared to have to answer more questions than just your name and address. Think about what they are advertising and what you have to offer. Be able to put yourself across in a succinct and businesslike manner.

There are more sophisticated versions where an organization develops comprehensive job descriptions and personnel specifications. These, together with data from job performance records, appraisals and termination interviews, help them to identify the handful of personal attributes or job experiences which indicate the type of person most likely to succeed. In other words they can draw up a weighted application or 'Biodata' format and use these together with a structured interview over the telephone.

One organization which uses this method recently received about 600 letters in response to a national advertisement. These were reduced to about 250 through the normal method of scrutiny against certain set criteria. The 250 applicants were then telephoned and invited to participate in the next stage of the selection procedure. They were asked to nominate a telephone number, a time and a day when they could prepare themselves for a conversation lasting about 30 to 40 minutes. Apart from Sundays and Saturday afternoons, any time of day up to about 10pm would be convenient to the organization. The applicant was also forewarned that they should find some private and quiet place. They should be prepared to answer questions about their work experiences and themselves – as they might have to do in a face-to-face interview. They were also asked to provide themselves with paper and pencil to make notes of some of the job conditions, etc. The telephone interviews took place as agreed and a final shortlist of about 60 applicants was arrived at. The organization felt that conducting 250, thirty-minute, structured telephone conversations was more cost-effective and productive than inviting the same number of people along for face-to-face interviews.

The same type of tactic may be used on you. Be prepared. You will have time to do some homework. When on the phone, speak clearly. Do not be afraid to ask the caller to repeat any question which is unclear. (Ask them to call back if it is a poor line.) Treat the caller as you would someone you meet face-to-face – with courtesy. Your demeanour during the conversation will be taken into account when the decision whether or not to include you in the final shortlist is being made. You should also be prepared to declare at the end of the conversation whether or not you are still interested in the vacancy.

What you should always remember to do

Whatever interview structure is used or whatever the style of the interviewers, you should always try to remember certain points. Here is a long list of Do's – and a shorter one of Don'ts – which are worth using as refreshers before your interview:

Interview checklist – do

- Do your homework.
- Plan your timetable.
- Arrive in sufficient time.
- Come well prepared.
- Dress appropriately – smart and well-presented.
- Make a good, confident entrance.
- Make eye contact.
- Smile.
- Shake hands firmly.
- Respect normal courtesies.
- You are on the interviewers' territory – don't make yourself too much 'at home' unless invited to do so and don't take over or invade their space.
- Behave appropriately for the situation.
- Be natural, smile and nod responsively when appropriate.
- Listen carefully, attentively and actively to what they are asking and saying.
- Listen to what they are not saying.
- Ensure you get your fair share of 'air time' – at least half.
- Speak clearly and loudly enough to be heard.
- Address your replies to the questioner by name if possible.
- Be self assured but not 'cocky'.
- Be honest and truthful.

- Take things seriously but demonstrate a sense of humour.
- Temper enthusiasm with dignity.
- Be factual about your achievements and don't denigrate yourself.
- Try to retain an alert body position with sufficient mobility to display interest and enthusiasm but avoid being thought 'a fidget'.
- Gesticulate when it helps support what you are saying.
- Stay warm and friendly even when under attack.
- Only volunteer positive information about yourself and answer questions in a clear, positive manner.
- Tell them what sort of work you enjoy and why, and the benefits this has for them, your job performance and the people with whom you work.
- Tell them about any additional skills you have which are not essential in terms of the job description but can be desirable and advantageous for the organization.
- Talk about the challenges the work offers.
- Keep highlighting your relevant experiences, achievements and contributions to other organizations.
- Watch out for signals that the interviewer wants to ask you something.
- Be sensitive to the interviewers' body language and the messages they are conveying.
- Try to 'mirror' their body language to increase rapport between you.
- Usually interpret their silences as a request for you to continue.
- Have a few questions to ask about the organization, the work, the conditions and the future.
- Look for signs that the interview is coming to a close.
- Ask about what happens next and when you might hear.

- Think about writing to the organization afterwards.
- Review your interview immediately afterwards.

Interview checklist – don't

- Chew gum during a conversation – it is uncouth!
- Smoke or eat unless invited to do so.
- Worry about being nervous – they probably are too.
- Correct the interviewers – unless you can do it very tactfully.
- Make negative judgements about yourself, your life and your achievements.
- Criticize the organization, the interviewers or the procedure.
- Tell the interviewers you can do everything, revolutionize their organization, spot all of their inefficiencies, and exceed the performance of all existing employees.
- Expect your words alone to sell you.
- Give up hope if the interviewer starts to put you down.
- Bore them.
- Bite the hands that have fed you.
- Put them on the spot by asking how well you have done – see if they raise it as part of their normal procedure.
- Talk about salary and packages unless they raise these matters – when you should know what you need, what you want and what you feel you are worth.

Multiple assessment centres

Assessment centres, together with the use of tests of ability and aptitude and personality questionnaires, are probably the fastest growing method of assessing people for employment. This is particularly true of appointments at graduate, sales, supervisory and managerial levels as well as for key professional jobs. They are increasingly used in larger organizations for selecting people for promotion or assessing their development needs. At least one police force uses them for all external recruitment and transfers from other forces, and the Services use it for officer selection. It is important that you understand what this method entails because the likelihood of you having to experience one is increasing.

In their present form, assessment centre techniques are probably less than 30 years old. They were used by the Americans during World War II to select 'spies' or agents. Their history also includes use by the War Office Selection Boards (WOSB) for officers entering the Armed Forces. They emerged into British industry after World War II under the guise of 'Group Selection'.

Multiple assessment centres share common features. You would be invited together with a small group of other candidates to the same venue at the same time. This might be an isolated location where you would have to stay overnight, sometimes stretching to two or three days. Here you would undertake a variety of activities selected from:

- individual case studies;
- completing the contents of a hypothetical manager's 'in-tray' as part of a decision-making and planning exercise;
- role-playing – especially of work-related activities like dealing with a difficult employee in a 'mock' interview;
- personal introduction to assessors and/or other candidates;
- a battery of psychological tests and questionnaires;
- 'managing' a small group of people who have a specific practical task to accomplish with limited resources in a short space of time and possibly out of doors;
- working with others as a team on a business simulation in competition with other teams;
- preparing and presenting a business proposal;
- participating in a leaderless group discussion with others who may have been briefed to have views different to your own;
- written problem-solving exercises;
- face-to-face interviews with individuals or panels;
- psychiatric assessment (especially for the Forces).

The most extensive assessment centres will include many of the above. An increasing number of organizations are now incorporating some of these activities into one-day extended selection procedures – a form of mini assessment centre.

When a university was appointing a new lecturer, applicants were forewarned that they would have to give a short prepared lecture or presentation to an audience composed of the assessors and the other candidates. This activity was to be in addition to the normal panel interview. The subject would be one of their choice but related to the syllabus they would have to teach if appointed.

An international manufacturing organization was appointing a new Management Training and Development Officer. Applicants were forewarned that, as well as being interviewed, they would also have to undertake some other activities. These would include sitting a battery of psychological tests, giving a short lecture on a relevant subject which would be revealed to them half an hour before it was to be presented to the assessors, completing a questionnaire on different training techniques and undertaking a written training needs analysis case study.

A large national supermarket chain were appointing trainee managers from a group of graduates. Candidates were invited to interview and asked also to complete some tests of ability and a personality questionnaire. They were also confronted with a member of the interviewing team who played the role of an irate customer with whom they had to deal there and then. In addition, they were given a short written employee relations disciplinary problem and were asked to write down how they would deal with it and the words they would use with the errant employee.

The rationale behind the Assessment Centre approach is simple: evidence collected about you from several sources is likely to be more reliable and valid than that obtained from the face-to-face interview alone. The introduction of several trained observers also helps to increase assessor reliability.

The sort of factors assessed by this procedure could include your:

- ability to grow and learn;
- ability to delegate;

- applied intellect;
- capacity to work under pressure;
- communication and presentation skills;
- decision-making skills;
- emotional stability;
- imagination and creativity;
- interpersonal and influencing skills;
- leadership skills;
- maturity;
- motivation;
- numerical ability;
- organizing ability;
- planning skills;
- practical judgement;
- problem-solving;
- resilience;
- time- and self-management;
- verbal ability.

Don't be surprised if you are invited to an interview and discover that there are also some additional activities 'tagged on' to make the day into a 'mini' assessment centre or an extended selection procedure. You might have to give a presentation or prepare a committee-type 'paper' to present to the final interviewing panel. A reasonable organization would forewarn you of these activities in their invitation. Some may even advise you of the dimensions they are going to assess.

Assessment centres are costly both to design and run. It is more likely that only larger organizations have the resources to use them regularly. Medium-sized or smaller companies may join forces to use this method. Alternatively they may select two or three of the activities and add them to their traditional interview. Some consultancies offer an assessment centre service. They will tailor-make a procedure for an organization or adapt one of their 'off-the-shelf' packages. The signs are that the practice is becoming more widespread.

Despite the initial costs of setting them up and their subsequent running costs, many organizations claim it is money well invested which can be recouped. One poor selection decision at a middle or senior management level can quite easily incur high costs – both financial and human. These could quite easily be far greater than the costs incurred in establishing what is felt to be a more valid and reliable method of assessment for that level of appointment.

The results from a number of assessment centre techniques can be statistically accumulated. These have been shown to produce higher reliability and validity than those normally obtained from one or two techniques – especially the face-to-face interview.

Assessment centres can be stimulating and good fun. They can also be very intensive and emotionally and intellectually draining. Above all, they can be very rewarding – especially if the organization is prepared to give you personal, confidential feedback on your performance. You might not get the job but you can get some invaluable 'input on your output' which can only improve your future performance if you act on the advice given.

Assessment centre checklist

It would be easy to be cynical if you fail an assessment centre and blame the 'shrinks' for their antics. But my advice is to think positively about the opportunity and:

- don't sit there doing nothing – participate;
- don't criticize the activity – get stuck in to it;
- keep to the point and persuade others to do so;
- see if you can encourage others to contribute;
- make sure you get a chance to make your point;
- don't try to 'hog' the proceedings – especially just by talking about anything in a loud voice;
- avoid putting down other people – comment on their ideas and not them as individuals;
- try not to fly off the handle – stay cool – engage brain before opening mouth;
- retain your sense of humour;
- always try to give of your best – you can do no more.

The implications for you as a result of what is happening in the area of selection is that interviewers will become more professional, interviews more structured and additional tactics such as assessment centres will be used. More structured interviewing could reduce your opportunity to provide information about yourself outside the questions they have decided to ask you. But the quality of your responses will still be under your control. Preparation will still be essential to ensure you promote yourself in the best possible light. Assessment centres will make selection more demanding but could be fairer in the long run and depend less upon the prejudices found in the traditional interview.

6 How can I improve my performance?

'They say best men are moulded out of faults,
And for the most, become much more the better for being a little bad.'

Measure for Measure Act V, Scene I
William Shakespeare

After the interview you are either going to get an offer of employment or be rejected. We shall look briefly at how to cope with the latter, but the main focus of this chapter is how to look positively at what you have learned about yourself and your interview behaviour which will help you to improve your performance next time.

Coping with rejection

Being rejected can have a very powerful affect on your self-esteem and motivation. For some it can range from being a momentary to a longer-lasting disappointment, whilst for others it becomes a spur to even greater efforts. You should always ensure, however, that you are not merely redoubling your efforts in the same wrong direction. A little thought is essential before 'girding up your loins'. Your endeavours must be both effective and efficient: you must first of all go after the right jobs and then use the right methods.

If you are rejected after a 'screening' or final interview, it is vital that you sit and reflect on the experience and see what you can learn from it which will help you to improve your future performance. You will rarely be told why you have been rejected in any form which will help you to improve your technique. The 'Dear John . . .' letters are very non-committal for a variety of reasons.

You could try telephoning the Personnel Department, the chairman of the panel or the manager who had the vacancy and ask for advice. Many are reluctant to tell you why you failed other than in very general terms. A few days after the interview they may even have forgotten which one you were! Some will also be concerned that what starts as an enquiry from you about your performance ends up with them being taken to an industrial tribunal for unlawful discrimination.

Something else you must seriously address is to whom or what do you attribute your lack of success? Do you feel that it is not your fault but that of 'the others' – the interviewers? Or is it the location or day or circumstances or what? Perhaps you feel that you just don't have any luck? If you see everyone else's good fortune as being based on luck or being in the right place at the right time, then you are probably lost! Many people who succeed have devoted a lot of their time and energy to making things happen for them. If it is luck, then you should see how you can go and get yourself some. If it is not, then what is it that they do or say or the ways they behave which helps them to get what they want out of life?

Improving your performance

Mildred was undoubtedly a highly capable academic but she did not make a very good first impression on academic appointment and promotion panels. According to a few of her valued friends she came across as an over-effusive, gushy, talkative person who 'rabbited on' and tended to refer to panel members as 'my dear'. She had problems with her feet which were solved at work by wearing sandals or very casual shoes and trousers. Her friends apprised her of these first impressions as tactfully as they could. She turned up at her next panel interview dressed in a smart business suit with matching accessories and wearing shoes. She moderated the behaviour raised by her colleagues . . . and got the job! Whilst personality might not change, behaviour can be changed if there's something in it for you!

Every interview should be a learning experience – whether or not you get the job – but more importantly when you do not! Here is an exercise to help you to learn from a less-successful interview.

Post-interview self-analysis

Write down some key words which best describe how you felt after the interview. Give specific reasons why you felt like that. Explain why you feel you did less well. Try to be specific. Go through your analysis and rehearse what you should have done or said – or how you think you would tackle these questions if you meet them in the future. Did you really prepare for that interview or hope that it would be 'all right on the night'?

If you want some ideas on how to do this analysis, read the following list of characteristics. Some of them may be more relevant to one interview rather than another. Tick those which you consider you lack and which may have let you down during the interview in question. Keep the list down to about ten to start with:

Achievement motivation	Adaptability	Ambition
Analytical skills	Appearance	Commitment
Composure	Conciseness	Curiosity
Decisiveness	Enthusiasm	Friendliness
Humility	Humour	Literacy
Lucidity	Maturity	Mobility
Neatness	Numeracy	Objectivity
Openness	Optimism	Organization
Persistence	Persuasiveness	Physique
Practical skills	Preparation	Qualifications
Self-confidence	Self-reliance	Sensitivity
Tolerance	Varied interests	Work experience

(The above exercise reprinted with permission from *Job Hunting: a definitive guide* published by the Centre for Self Development, Leamington Spa.)

Self-motivation and action planning

Being rejected can have a debilitating effect on your self-esteem – if you let it. Avoiding rejection is easy – do nothing! If you want to make changes in your life you must do something and there will be inevitable disappointments. You are capable of rising above these. It takes some people longer than others to cope with not succeeding at an interview. You have to learn to 'pick yourself up, dust yourself off and start all over again!' Easier said than done, you say? Life is rarely a smooth upward movement in which you get every job for which you apply. Take a positive outlook by treating every situation as a learning opportunity. Ask yourself:

'What did I do well?'
Because rarely is everything bad!

'What could I do better?'
And you have some ideas now on how to do this.

'Who might I talk to help improve my technique?'
As part of your preparation for your next interview, see if you can talk to a friend and get help from them in undertaking a 'mock' interview. Try not to let your frustration build up inside you. Talk it through with someone in a positive manner. Even doing something physically demanding will help to dissipate your emotional energy – sports, gardening, leisure pursuits, etc.

You might have to consider getting some independent, objective advice. Friends and family may be able to help here – but it can be tricky for someone who is close to you or with whom there are ties of friendship. Perhaps it would be worthwhile paying for some form of vocational or career assessment? This could be a day's career counselling or more comprehensive outplacement services lasting several weeks, which would typically include assistance with letter writing, CV preparation, company research, interviewing and self-presentation skills.

The number of people who do insufficient preparation could be quite large. The gap for you between your present performance and future success may be small. You could easily place yourself well up 'the field' with a little extra effort. Try it and good luck.

Index

Other Titles in the Business Matters Series

Effective Leadership
A practical guide to leading your team to success
Malcolm Bird

The Business of Assertiveness
A practical guide to being more effective in the work place
Rennie Fritchie and Maggie Melling

Negotiating: Everybody Wins
A practical guide to negotiation in your work place and home
Vanessa Helps

Speak for Yourself
A practical guide to speaking with confidence
John Campbell

Give and Take
A practical guide to making the most of meetings
Jack Gratus

Managing Pressure at Work
A practical guide to managing time and other pressures and for coping with stress
Helen Froggatt and Paul Stamp

How Do You Manage?
How to make the most of yourself and your people
John Nicholson